BUTTRESSES OF A WILD-FIG TREE SEEN THROUGH BAMBOO STEMS IN CENTRAL BELIZE

A HALO OF CLOUDS AROUND GUATEMALA'S VOLCAN DE AGUA

NESTING RIDLEY TURTLES AT NANCITE BEACH, COSTA RICA

PINE SAVANNA NEAR MATAGALPA IN THE NICARAGUAN HIGHLANDS

MANGROVE- AND PALM-CLAD CAYS OFF BELIZE AT SUNDOWN

TREE FERNS AND PHILODENDRONS IN THE MONTE VERDE CLOUD FOREST, COSTA RICA

A SHALLOW INLET BEHIND CAHUITA POINT, COSTA RICA

Other Publications:

CENTRAL AMERICAN JUNGLES

THE AMERICAN WILDERNESS/TIME-LIFE BOOKS/ALEXANDRIA, VIRGINIA

BY DON MOSER
AND THE EDITORS OF TIME-LIFE BOOKS

WITH PHOTOGRAPHS BY CO RENTMEESTER

Time-Life Books Inc.
is a wholly owned subsidiary of

TIME INCORPORATED

FOUNDER: Henry R. Luce 1898-1967

Editor-in-Chief: Henry Anatole Grunwald
President: J. Richard Munro
Chairman of the Board: Ralph P. Davidson
Executive Vice President: Clifford J. Grum
Chairman, Executive Committee: James R. Shepley
Editorial Director: Ralph Graves
Group Vice President, Books: Joan D. Manley
Vice Chairman: Arthur Temple

TIME-LIFE BOOKS INC.

EDITOR: George Constable
Executive Editor: George Daniels
Board of Editors: Dale M. Brown, Thomas H. Flaherty Jr.;
Martin Mann, Philip W. Payne, John Paul Porter,
Gerry Schremp, Gerald Simons, Nakanori Tashiro,
Kit van Tulleken
Planning Director: Edward Brash
Art Director: Tom Suzuki
   Assistant: Arnold C. Holeywell
Director of Administration: David L. Harrison
Director of Operations: Gennaro C. Esposito
Director of Research: Carolyn L. Sackett
   Assistant: Phyllis K. Wise
Director of Photography: Dolores Allen Littles

President: Carl G. Jaeger
Executive Vice Presidents: John Steven Maxwell,
David J. Walsh
Vice Presidents: George Artandi, Stephen L. Bair,
Peter G. Barnes, Nicholas Benton, John L. Canova,
Beatrice T. Dobie, Carol Flaumenhaft, James L. Mercer,
Herbert Sorkin, Paul R. Stewart

THE AMERICAN WILDERNESS

EDITOR: Robert Morton
Editorial Staff for *Central American Jungles*
Picture Editor: Patricia Hunt
Designer: Charles Mikolaycak
Staff Writers: Marion Buhagiar, Carol Clingan
Chief Researcher: Martha T. Goolrick
Researchers: Reese Hassig, Beatrice Hsia,
Trish Kiesewetter, Ellie McGrath, Editha Yango
Design Assistant: Vincent Lewis
Copy Coordinator: Susan Tribich
Picture Coordinator: Joan Lynch

Revisions Staff
SENIOR EDITOR: Rosalind Stubenberg
Chief Researcher: Barbara Levitt
Text Editor: Lee Greene
Researcher: Martha Reichard George
Copy Coordinator: Cynthia Kleinfeld
Art Assistant: Jeanne Potter
Editorial Assistants: Mary Kosak, Linda Yates

Editorial Operations
Production Director: Feliciano Madrid
   Assistants: Peter A. Inchauteguiz, Karen A. Meyerson
Copy Processing: Gordon E. Buck
Quality Control Director: Robert L. Young
   Assistant: James J. Cox
   Associates: Daniel J. McSweeney, Michael G. Wight
Art Coordinator: Anne B. Landry
Copy Room Director: Susan Galloway Goldberg
   Assistants: Celia Beattie, Ricki Tarlow

The Author: Don Moser has been in love with wild country since his boyhood. He has worked as a fire lookout and ranger naturalist in the American West, later explored wilderness areas in Southeast Asia, and for this book spent seven months in Central America. A former writer, bureau chief and assistant managing editor for *Life*, Moser is now the editor of *Smithsonian*. He is author of *The Snake River Country* in this series; *The Peninsula*, a book about Olympic National Park; and a novel entitled *A Heart to the Hawks*.

The Photographer: A *Life* photographer for many years, Co Rentmeester tramped the jungles of Southeast Asia with Don Moser when both were covering the Vietnam War. Rentmeester received numerous awards for his pictures on a variety of subjects and was named Magazine Photographer of the Year for his coverage of the 1972 Olympics. Born in the Netherlands, he was an Olympic athlete himself, representing his country on its rowing team in Rome in 1960. Rentmeester's work appears in many international publications, and he has published a book of his photographs of Indonesia.

The Cover: A green wall of ferns and vine-draped trees lines the bank of a rain-forest stream in the Guatemalan lowlands. The dearth of small plants on the stream's muddy margins testifies to the fluctuation in the water level; much of the area's 100 inches of annual rain falls in July and October.

CORRESPONDENTS: Elisabeth Kraemer (Bonn); Margot Hapgood, Dorothy Bacon, Lesley Coleman (London); Susan Jonas, Lucy T. Voulgaris (New York); Maria Vincenza Aloisi, Josephine du Brusle (Paris); Ann Natanson (Rome). Valuable assistance was also provided by: Stewart Krohn (Belize); Robert Kroon (Geneva); Karen Bates (Guatemala); Karin B. Pearce (London); Paolo Bosio, Willi Germund (Managua); Laura López, Simon Walker (Mexico); Carolyn T. Chubet, Miriam Hsia, Christina Lieberman (New York); Mimi Murphy (Rome); Teresa Ponte (Tegucigalpa).

For information about any Time-Life book, please write:
Reader Information
Time-Life Books
541 North Fairbanks Court
Chicago, Illinois 60611

Library of Congress Cataloguing in Publication Data
Moser, Don.
   Central American jungles / by Don Moser and the editors of
Time-Life Books; with photos. by C. Rentmeester.—New York:
Time-Life Books, c1975.
   184 p. : ill. (some col.); 27 cm.—(The American wilderness)
   Bibliography: p. 180.
   Includes index.
   1. Natural history—Central America.
   I. Rentmeester, Co.   II. Time-Life Books.   III. Title.
QH108.A1M67   500.9'728   75-14284
ISBN 0-8094-1344-2
ISBN 0-8094-1343-3 (lib. bdg.)
ISBN 0-8094-1342-6 (retail ed.)

TIME-LIFE is a trademark of Time Incorporated U.S.A.

Contents

The Meeting Ground of the Americas

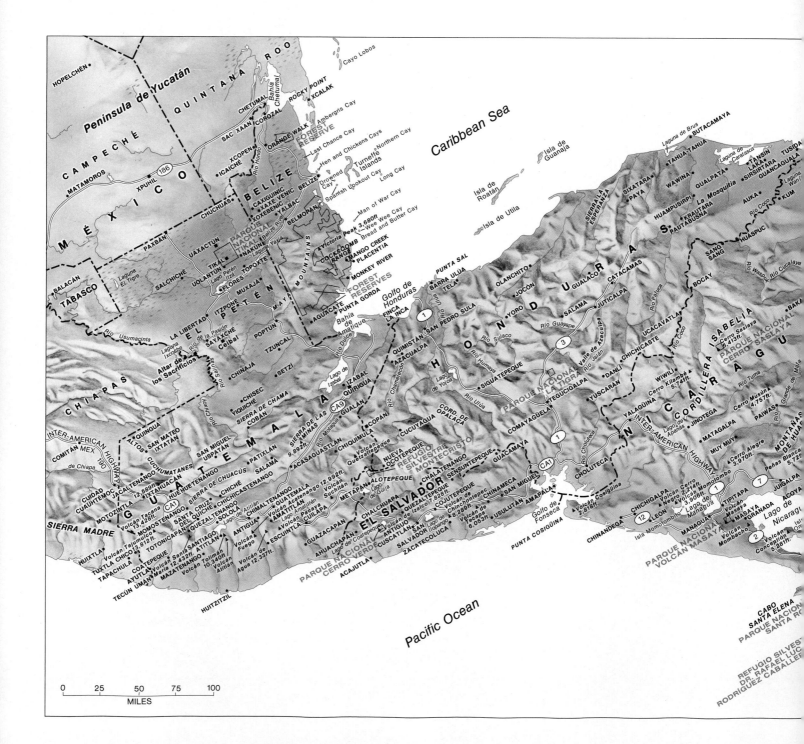

Pacific Ocean

Caribbean Sea

0   25   50   75   100
MILES

Nurtured by the tropic sun and by moisture from sea winds, the great intercontinental bridge called Central America is a land of surpassing diversity. Volcanoes rise from jungles; tangled swamps adjoin silken-smooth beaches. Seven countries share the narrow corridor, where the flora and fauna of both abutting land masses mingle—kinkajous of the south with raccoons of the north, equatorial orchids with temperate-zone pines. From the coastal rain forest of Belize, along the flanks of the Great Divide and down to Darién in Panama, the region embraces vast tracts of wilderness.

On the map below, red lines mark nationally protected parks, preserves and a major archeological site in Guatemala; black squares mark other important Maya ruins. Swamps are shown by blue dashes; black triangles indicate volcanoes and other peaks. The Inter-American Highway as well as other major roads in the region are shown as numbered white lines.

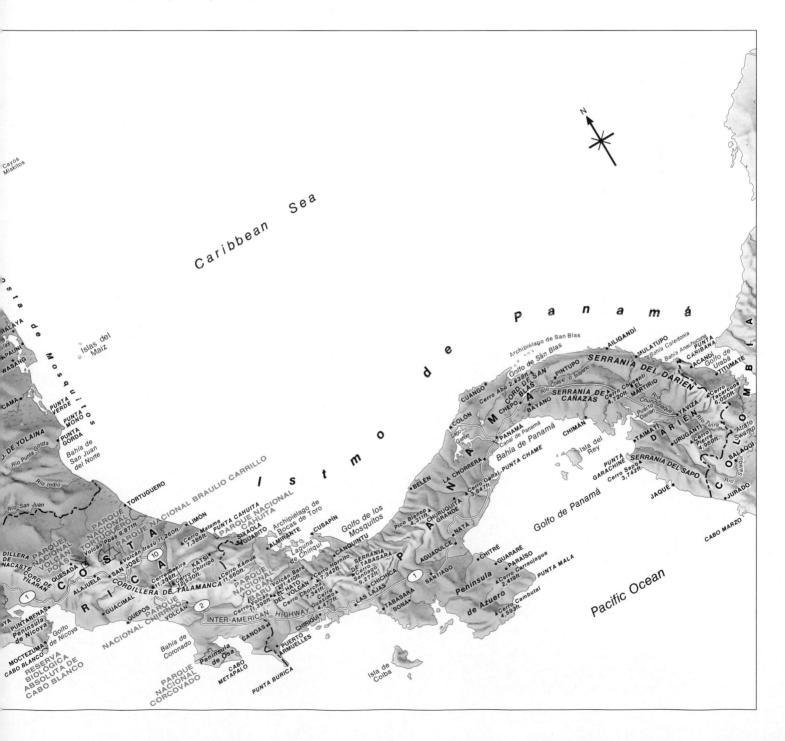

1/ A Bridge between Continents

Sun-flooded, high-rising, rain-wet . . . a causeway and asylum for migrating hosts of the world's live things, laid out and sculptured just right to show the vast potential of the tropics. ARCHIE CARR/ NATURE AND THE FUTURE OF CENTRAL AMERICA

At the first light of dawn the *guardabarrancas* started singing all up and down the mountainside. I had never seen one of these elusive little birds—the "guards of the ravine"—but in the half-dark their tinkling song was very beautiful. For a while, as I lay listening to them, it sounded as if the jungle were ringing with a thousand wind chimes.

I crawled out of my sleeping bag and blew some flames back into the embers of last night's campfire. The air was cool here, high on the slopes of the dormant volcano, and I warmed myself by huddling over the fire. It had rained during the night, and drops of water sprinkled me as they fell from the forest canopy 100 feet above. In a few minutes the warden of the forest, Jesús Flores, came loping up the overgrown track, swinging his machete. Jesús is an Indian, a descendant of the Maya, and ordinarily solemn, but now a big grin split his face. As a rule he patrols the forest only on weekends; during the week he works on a coffee *finca,* a plantation lower on the slopes of the mountain. But today, a Monday, my presence gave him an excuse to spend the day prowling about in the forest and smoking my good gringo cigarettes, and he was clearly delighted.

We toasted tortillas over the fire and drank coffee as the sun got up and the *guardabarrancas* sang themselves inside out. When we finished breakfast, we strapped on a couple of water bottles and began to climb higher into the jungle. Jesús and I were at an altitude of about 6,000 feet on the flank of Guatemala's Volcán Atitlán, in a large tract of un-touched forest set aside as a preserve by some conservation-minded *finca* owners. This morning we were searching for a glimpse of a very rare and exceptionally beautiful bird called the resplendent trogon, or quetzal. The quetzal exists only in the sort of high, cool, wet forest we were now entering—an environment that scientists call montane rain forest or cloud forest. As either name suggests, it is a world frequently veiled in mists and thus appealingly mysterious, tantalizing in its hints of hidden beauty.

There was a trail of sorts, visible to Jesús if not to me. Jesús had warned me that if I went into the jungle alone I might through ig-norance step on the *ajo* vine, and that anyone who stepped on an *ajo* vine was bound to get lost. I did not share this belief in the magical prop-erties of the *ajo* vine, but I certainly accepted the principle. Alone, I would have been lost within minutes.

The jungle closed around us, green on green on green. The foliage was so dense that the eye had no point of reference. It was not until we stopped for a breather that I could actually see the forest in its com-ponent parts rather than in its baffling entirety. I sprawled on the moist volcanic soil and tried to make some sense out of the confusion of liv-ing matter that surrounded us. Nearby stood a big tree fern, a relic from the age of dinosaurs. Perhaps a dozen feet tall, the fern erupted into a spray of long delicate fronds and fiddleheads large enough to grace a cello. Above us on the slope was an extraordinary-looking tree with a trunk so tortured and twisted as to seem in agony. Jesús called it the *matapalo,* or tree killer—an apt name, for this tree was a strangler fig. Having grown up as a slender vine twined around another tree, the fig had eventually enveloped and killed its host; now the adult fig was a great free-standing tree in its own right.

Overhead, the larger branches of other trees were so festooned with plant life that it seemed they might come crashing down under the weight they supported. Growing along each branch were orchids, ferns, mosses and plants of a dozen other kinds; all of them were epiphytes, drawing their nourishment from the leaf litter that accumulated on the limb and from nutrients washed down the host tree by rain. On a branch directly above me was a bromeliad, a spiky-leafed epiphyte a couple of feet across. At the base of the diverging leaves, I knew, there would be a kind of natural tank filled with a few inches of rain water. There, 80 feet in the air, mosquito larvae and the tadpoles of arboreal frogs would be wriggling about. On the branches, in the crevices of trees, on the ground—wherever I looked there was hardly a foot of space that was not occupied. Every available niche was filled. Life here overlapped itself, layer on layer.

It was time to move on. We started climbing again; after a while, through a gap in the foliage, I could see mists beginning to swirl in against the flanks of the mountain just a few hundred feet above us, their tendrils snaking in among the trees. We kept climbing, up toward the clouds.

With its luxuriance, its complexity, its stupefying abundance of life, the cloud forest can serve well as a symbol for Central America as a whole. Although Central America is not large—in total area it is considerably smaller than the state of Texas—it joins two continents that are vastly different in character. There are few places on earth, consequently, where the forces of nature so actively and obviously interplay. The winds and weather of two great oceans meet above Central America's jungles and mountains. (Indeed, in parts of Panama the oceans lie only 50 miles apart, and there are places on the Atlantic shore from which it is possible to reach the Pacific coast by traveling due *east*.) Lying in a zone of great geological activity as well as in the path of tropical storms and hurricanes, Central America is subject to far more than an ordinary share of nature's rampages. All of these stresses and influences, applied to a small land mass, have resulted in a scene of remarkable richness and variety.

Central America consists of seven countries—Guatemala, El Salvador, Honduras, Nicaragua, Costa Rica, Panama and Belize, formerly known as British Honduras. The entire region lies within what scientists call the Neotropics—the tropics of the New World—but its climate and landscapes are by no means uniform. The Caribbean coast of Central America is low, hot and wet, a flat landscape where slanting monsoonal rains bow down the coconut palms and whip the mangrove-lined lagoons into froth. The Pacific side is drier and steeper; here a booming surf crashes against the beaches and rocky headlands, and the trees of the inland forests lose their leaves in the dry season, though not their spines and thorns.

Not far back from the Pacific coast a file of giant volcanoes marches down from Guatemala through El Salvador and on to Panama. In northern Guatemala, in the jungles of a region called the Petén, egrets fly up in white billows from sinuous, slow-moving streams, and six-foot iguanas dive into the water from overarching trees. In central Guatemala,

A male quetzal feeds on insects in a rotting tree in a Guatemalan cloud forest. As with most bird species, the male is showier than the female, which is the same shimmery green but lacks the male's long tail feathers and has a black rather than yellow bill.

pine-covered highlands that look as if they might have been transplant-ed from the foothills of the Rockies lie adjacent to arid valleys, where tall cactus stands against a hot, white sky. Farther south, in Honduras, rugged, densely forested mountains fall away toward gorges drained by steeply plunging rivers. In Nicaragua a huge inland sea populated by sharks and sawfish stretches over the horizon. In Costa Rica and Pan-ama, where the land begins to take on a feeling that is distinctly equatorial, the jungle's sudden dawns erupt with the explosive roars of howler monkeys.

The many fascinations of Central America stem from a single, sim-ple fact: Central America is a land bridge, linking a continent of the Northern Hemisphere and a radically different continent of the South-ern Hemisphere. But the story of how the bridge was formed, and how it came to serve as a passageway and meeting ground for all manner of plants and creatures, is not at all simple.

Hundreds of millions of years ago, all of the earth's major land masses were joined in a single world continent, which geologists call Pangaea. About 200 million years ago the world continent split into a northern and a southern land mass. The northern continent, Laurasia, consisted of what is now North America, Europe and Asia; the southern conti-nent, Gondwanaland, was made up of South America, Africa, Australia, India and Antarctica.

About 130 million years ago, South America separated from the rest of Gondwanaland and became, in effect, a gigantic island; its creatures, which included marsupials and edentates—precursors of today's sloths, anteaters and armadillos—developed in isolation. North America sep-arated from Eurasia much later; by then it was already well populated with the ancestors of our cats, dogs, rodents, weasels and other present-day mammals. It was also inhabited by monkeys, which had migrated from their original home in Africa up through Europe and into North America before the continental separation was complete.

For millions of years North and South America remained divided by hundreds of miles of ocean, and their fauna and flora took different evolutionary paths. But the earth's forces were to change all that.

The earth's surface is made up of a number of huge, rigid plates that are constantly moving in relation to one another. The thicker sections of the plates are the continents; the thinner parts make up the rock beneath the ocean floors. When two plates move toward each other, the result is geologic upheaval on a vast scale. Such an encounter occurred about 20 million years ago in the region between North and South America. The newly formed Cocos Plate, a relatively small one some 300 miles wide, moved eastward from the Pacific until it met the plate underlying the Caribbean. The eastern edge of the Cocos Plate was driven beneath the western edge of the Caribbean Plate. As the Cocos Plate was forced downward, the friction, as well as the heat deep within the earth, liquefied its rock into magma, which found release by thrusting up in a chain of volcanoes. The volcanic islands that resulted formed a line of stepping stones between the northern and southern continents.

Going from island to island—probably by traveling on mats of floating vegetation—the first mammals began to move back and forth between North and South America. The geologic record is incomplete —possibly the island chain sank beneath the sea and reemerged several times—but it is certain that during this period the rodents of North America reached the southern continent, and so did the monkeys; the monkeys found the tropical climate of South America to their liking and thrived there, while their cousins in the colder north died out.

As the Cocos Plate continued moving eastward and the friction between it and the Caribbean Plate increased, more volcanoes were thrust up and mountains began to rise from the sea. By three or four million years ago, an unbroken stretch of dry land had joined the continents. The Central American bridge was now open for business.

Mammals, birds, insects and reptiles began to pour across the bridge in both directions. The opossum headed north, ultimately reaching the Northern United States, where it still flourishes. A ground sloth the size of an elephant headed north too, and made it to the Southwest before it died out, perhaps the victim of early hunters. The armored nine-foot-long glyptodont also reached the United States and also died there—but its descendants still live in Texas and Florida in the form of smaller armadillos.

The big migration, however, was from north to south. The highly efficient mammals that had developed on the northern continent—cats, dogs, weasels and others—swarmed down the bridge into South America, where they soon came to dominate the environment, diversifying into forms more appropriate for the tropics.

Today, northern and southern cousins continue to meet along the Central American bridge. In Nicaragua a mountain lion and a jaguar snarl at each other from opposite banks of a stream. In a Belizean meadow the white-tailed deer familiar to northerners browses a short distance away from a little brocket deer of the South American jungles. In Guatemala a raccoon glances up from its meal and finds itself face to face with what looks like a streamlined fun-house-mirror version of itself—a coatimundi from the southland. In Costa Rica, a jungle traveler may encounter a North American rattlesnake in the morning and a South American bushmaster in the afternoon.

Essentially, temperate North America has thrust southward over the bridge along the cool slopes of the mountains and the flanks of the great volcanoes. Tropical South America has advanced northward along the hot lowlands of both coasts. In Central America, anyone who wants to journey, as it were, from an Amazonian jungle to a Midwestern oak forest can simply start in a valley and walk uphill. For a visitor from the United States, reminders of home are everywhere—not only in the tracks of a deer, but in a patch of scrub oaks on a prairie and in the birds that have flown in for the winter. Yet these reminders exist side by side with plants and creatures that are distinctly tropical. I remember once in Costa Rica when I spotted a bird that looked totally familiar. It was a black-cowled oriole, a yellower version of the Baltimore oriole; watching it, I felt comfortably at home. A moment later, I looked down at my feet and spotted a tiny bright-red frog, of the type from which South American Indians once extracted a deadly poison with which to tip their arrows.

With its startling contrasts and abundance of life forms, Central America is a wonderful place for someone who likes to poke around wild places and observe wild things. But a visitor from the north must be prepared for an experience very different from the sort that might previously have been encountered in Yosemite National Park, say, or on the Appalachian Trail. In Central America, except for a very few places like the Atitlán preserve, one does not find any major national parks or forests with carefully maintained trails and helpful rangers. At the same time, logging and the development of large-scale commercial agriculture have transformed much of Central America's wildest terrain. This is true particularly in the highlands, whose cool but moist environment is ideal not only for the growth of forests but for the production of coffee, tea and quinine. It is true also in the Pacific lowlands, where beef and cotton have become major products for export.

But out beyond the boundaries of human encroachment are areas so rugged they make the remotest parts of the United States seem civilized. These hinterlands have neither roads nor trails; only the most accomplished outdoorsmen can penetrate them without the assistance of local guides.

Certainly anyone who wants to enjoy the wild country of Central America must have an affinity for the jungle, for jungles of all kinds dominate the region all the way from the limestone plateaus of northern Guatemala to the swampy lowlands of eastern Panama. Biologists, who need to be precise, do not use the general term jungle. Instead they say "tropical rain forest" when referring to the lush growth of the Caribbean lowlands, "tropical deciduous forest" when talking about the seasonally dry bush of the Pacific slope, or "lower montane rain forest" when discussing the well-watered highlands. The forests differ in the kinds of plants and creatures they contain, but all have in common the luxuriance of vegetation usually associated with the word jungle.

Yet these Central American forests only superficially resemble the jungle of fiction and the movies—what might be called Tarzan's jungle. Tarzan's jungle is so impenetrable that no one can move through it without the ability to swing on vines. Ferocious animals lurk behind every tree, and overhanging branches drip with boa constrictors. Flowers the size of a man's head grow everywhere, and the air is filled with a constant cacophony of feral howls, screams and shrieks.

In the real jungles of Central America the foliage can indeed be so dense that one cannot move through it without a machete and a good arm; but often the shade cast by the leafy canopy of the taller trees keeps the undergrowth within bounds, so that one can walk through the forest with only moderate difficulty. Snakes certainly exist, and so do other creatures, but since vision is restricted by the foliage and most jungle animals are shy, they are rarely seen—and they seldom, if ever, attack. In fact, of all Central American mammals only the white-lipped peccary, a surly, sharp-tusked, piglike animal, which roams the jungle in bands of up to 50, is apt to be dangerous.

As for the fanciful foliage, there are indeed a few gaudy-flowering trees, but most jungle flowers are small and inconspicuous; of the 1,000-plus species of orchids in Costa Rica, the majority have tiny blossoms whose exquisite beauty is best appreciated with the aid of a hand lens. As for those jungle sounds, some birds utter cries that are weird beyond description, and the unexpected roar of a howler monkey is guaranteed to make a traveler's hair stand on end. Much of the time, however, the jungle is eerily silent.

The real jungles are hot—although not necessarily so hot as one might expect. For example, the jungles of Panama, deep within the tropics, do not have extremely high temperatures. The reason for this has to do

The broad leaves of a heliconia, a member of the banana family, thrust up through a tangle of ferns and vines in the Atitlán cloud forest.

with Panama's proximity to the equator, the line around the earth's midsection where the sun remains almost directly overhead for most of the year. But even as the sun beats down at its maximum intensity, a cooling effect takes place to moderate the extreme heat. As the heated air rises almost straight upward, it is replaced by cooler air from the oceans nearby. Farther to the north or south this phenomenon is not as effective: The sun's rays fall cruelly on ground that never has an opportunity to cool. Thus the earth's great deserts and zones of extreme heat tend to be located near the borders of the tropics, rather than directly along the equator. In the central part of Panama, which lies only nine degrees north of the equator, temperatures in the 80s and low 90s are common throughout the year, but the 100°-plus summer temperatures common in Mexico's southern Chihuahuan desert, hundreds of miles to the north, are unheard of.

If the jungles of Central America are not quite so hot as one might expect, they *are* as humid—thanks to their moisture-trapping forest canopies. In Costa Rican and Panamanian lowland jungles, the relative humidity hovers between 95 and 99 per cent. For people who are not well acclimated, the briefest walk on a trail leaves their clothing saturated with sweat and their faces steaming like boiled-over radiators. Virtually overnight, molds and fungi appear on everything, including the human body. There is even a fungus that flourishes inside binoculars and eats away the protective coating on the lenses.

The jungle holds other discomforts the traveler must be prepared to accept. I quickly learned—the hard way—never to sit down on anything or lean against anything or put a hand on anything, at least not without looking first. Many trees and shrubs bear thorns as big and sharp as darning needles; others have poisonous spines or nettles that can produce a painful rash. A legion of small biting and stinging creatures—spiders, ticks—are waiting to crawl up a pant leg or down inside a shirt, and though local people and seasoned jungle hands often build up an immunity to them, most newcomers are sensitive to their attacks.

Of all these creatures, my own worst foes are the tiny, ferocious mites called chiggers, which abound in some parts of the jungle. Chiggers bore into the flesh, liquefy the tissues with secretions and dine on the resulting liquid. Their bites swell into hard lumps that itch fiercely for days. In Panama, each morning I armored myself against chiggers as thoroughly as if I were going to a joust. First I dusted my legs with sulfur powder, which I had heard was a superb insect repellent. Then I stuffed my trousers into my boots and wrapped the junction between boots and pants with heavy tape. Finally I sprayed myself thoroughly with a second powerful insect repellent. But the chiggers penetrated these barriers so easily that I might as well have been walking about the jungle naked, and within a few days my legs were covered with bloody welts. As for the sulfur powder, once in Costa Rica I opened my sack of the stuff and out sashayed a scorpion.

Yet, for some people, and I am one of them, the tropical forests have an allure that abates discomforts—and that cannot be matched by anything in the temperate zones. There is rare beauty, the mystery of things unseen, the sense of life at flood tide. There is a kind of jungle fever that infects the blood: once stricken, the victim is drawn back again and again to the world that lies within the green walls.

On the morning that I climbed with Jesús Flores up into the cloud forest of Atitlán, I indulged myself in a futile pastime, which I had taken to practicing in other jungles: I tried to learn to identify the trees. Each time we passed a tree I would ask Jesús what it was called, and he would reply with the Spanish or Indian name. We passed a spongy-barked tree with oval leaves, which Jesús called a *zapotillo;* then a smooth-barked tree with lance-shaped leaves, which he called an *uzuxte.* Next came a gray-barked tree hanging with lianas—a *chicarro* —and a small shrubby tree known as *limoncillo.* A muscly trunked tree that reminded me of hornbeam was a *palo escobo,* and a tree with clusters of vicious-looking thorns along its trunk was a *palo corona.* A particularly large and majestic tree—perhaps 100 feet tall—was a *mescal.* Each tree we passed was of a different species, and after a while I began to lose track of them. By the time we reached the *mescal,* I had already forgotten which tree was the *zapotillo.*

Even after half a year in Central America, I was still confused by the trees in the forest. Indeed, one of the most important differences between nature in the tropics and in the temperate zones is, in the words of the biologists, "species richness." To put it simply: there are more kinds of living things in the tropics—many, many more kinds. A patch of a few hundred acres of Illinois countryside might contain 25 or 30 species of trees. An equivalent tract in a tropical forest might contain 400 species. And this multiplicity is true not only of plants, but of almost all life forms. In the tropics there are more kinds of birds, insects, reptiles, mammals. Take bats, for example. In the state of Ohio there are only about 10 species of bats, all of which live on insects. In Costa Rica, which is much smaller than Ohio, there are over 100 species of bats, not only insectivorous bats but bats that drink nectar, bats that catch fish, bats that eat papaya and other fruit, bats that eat other bats —even bats that drink the blood of deer.

Along with species richness, tropical forests are characterized by the wide dispersal of species, particularly plant species. This, too, is a contrast to temperate zone forests, which divide themselves rather neatly into distinctive plant neighborhoods according to soil type, drainage, the stage of plant succession and other factors. The neighborhoods are easily recognized, comfortably homogeneous. Up on the ridge, for example, is the white-oak neighborhood, where all the white oaks live. Down in the ravine is hemlock town, where the hemlocks stand companionably, side by side. Along the stream is willowville, where the willows grow so close you can hardly force your way between them. But in a tropical forest one might pass a lone cecropia tree, then not see another cecropia for several hundred yards. In between the two are a hundred other tree species—and often only one of each.

The diversity of species, even for such a natural meeting ground as a land bridge, makes Central America especially intriguing to any wilderness traveler. However, it also raises a nagging question: why? Not why is there so much living stuff; Central America's climate is hot and wet, and one would expect a great deal of life in such a greenhouse environment. But why life in such incredible variety?

The answer to this question is still the subject of research and lively debate among biologists. Of the theories that have been advanced, the most logical and fascinating to me is that species richness—or the lack of it—has to do with the availability of protein in the environment.

Nearly all living things require protein, the raw material for the building of tissue and the creation of enzymes. Protein is made up of amino acids, which plants make when they combine nitrogen from nitrates in the soil with carbon, hydrogen and oxygen from the air. Animals cannot manufacture these basic amino acids; they can obtain them only by eating plants, or by eating animals that have eaten plants.

But most vegetable matter is not rich in protein; mature plants are made up primarily of carbohydrates. Protein is found only in seeds, fruits, growing shoots, young leaves and the living cambium layer of the trunk or stem.

In temperate ones, when spring days get long and there is sufficient sunlight for growth to begin, a so-called protein pulse occurs, during which billions of plants burst forth with protein-rich buds, shoots and young leaves. For a short time, there is a protein surplus, almost a protein glut. The rhythms of animal life are keyed closely to this period of protein availability. The eggs of insects, dormant over the winter, hatch and loose their hordes. Birds return from the south, raise their broods and triple or quadruple their numbers within weeks. Frogs and toads crawl from hibernation in the mud and lay eggs by the thousands. Larger mammals, with a perfect genetic understanding of the protein cycle, have timed their couplings in the preceding fall or winter so that they now bring forth their young in a period of protein abundance.

For a few weeks, increasing numbers of animals gobble up all the protein they can get. And there are so many leaves and shoots, all appearing simultaneously, that the plants' survival is not itself threatened.

With the onset of summer the protein surplus passes. But now that the animals' young have grown, and all those bodies have been built, the need for protein has slackened. And predation and disease have already begun to cut into the animal population. By late summer and early fall, the survivors must prepare for the hard times of winter, when there will be little food. Fortunately, the plants now provide a second food pulse in the form of berries, seeds and nuts that contain protein, sugar and fats. In the waning weeks of summer, birds are able to pack in food to sustain them during their flight south and animals are able to prepare for the adversities of winter.

Thus, in the temperate zones the natural world is geared to the cyclic availability of protein. But in the tropics, the seasonal cycle is by no means as pronounced as in temperate climates. The days are of approximately the same length throughout the year; there is always sufficient sunlight for plant growth, and it is always reasonably warm. Freed from bondage to the sun's cycle, plants germinate, grow, flower and seed every month of the year. But while there is always some protein around, there is never a distinct protein surplus, never the equivalent of a northern spring where every tree and shrub within hundreds of miles is pouring out protein all at the same time. Nor is it easy for tropical plants to build protein in large quantities. The nitrate-rich leaf litter on the forest floor decomposes quickly in tropical heat; the nitrates are leached out and washed away by heavy rains before growing plants can seize them.

Since the plants have to work hard to generate new growth, they cannot afford to have their young shoots and leaves devoured by ravening hordes of insects, birds and mammals. To protect themselves, tropical plants have developed a wide variety of stratagems. Some sprout spines and thorns, others exude toxic resins or produce fruits filled with deadly poisons. A tree may put out a single new leaf today, another tomorrow, a third the day after that, never exposing too much of its new growth to predation at any one time. Trees of the same species within the same forest may flower and fruit at widely different times and intervals, totally out of synchronization with each other, as if to prevent animals from anticipating their availability as food.

Thus the intense competition for their shoots, new leaves and fruits has pressured tropical plants to diversify. For the same reason they also disperse. A hundred trees of a given species, standing on the same acre and fruiting at the same time, would be apt to have all their fruits eaten by a single band of peccaries; if the same hundred trees are spread over a square mile, at least some of them will remain undiscovered. If any plant species starts to become clearly dominant—as is characteristic of temperate-zone forests—the predators will discover the food bonanza, swarm in and quickly thin out the dominant plant.

The evolutionary thrust in the tropics, then, is toward varying species, widely dispersed. It might be said that the plants "want" to be different from one another, in order to avoid being devoured.

As Central America's plants have diversified, so have its animals. Because plant protein is scarce at any given time, and because the plants have evolved stratagems to guard it, animals are forced to compete fiercely for the available protein. This competition has influenced the form that tropical animals take. For one thing, they tend to be small. The largest mammal in Central America is the tapir, a long-snouted, leathery-hided beast that weighs up to 700 pounds. But tapirs have never been numerous; there is simply not enough protein in the jungle to build large numbers of big bodies. A few Central American animals have solved the protein problem by becoming virtually omnivorous. An example is the howler monkey. The howler's complex stomach is populated with bacteria that help to break down otherwise indigestible food. The howler is a kind of arboreal goat, capable of eating just about anything that grows.

But the great majority of the animals in Central America have survived by becoming accomplished specialists in seeking out and obtaining food of a particular type, staking claims to narrow ecological niches in which other creatures are not able to compete with them. Thus Central America's roster includes a common butterfly, *Heliconius*, whose caterpillar subsists on the leaves of a plant so filled with cyanide that any human who ate a pound of the foliage would drop dead, and

Clusters of unripe fruit dangle from a papaya tree in Panama. A favorite food of hungry travelers in the jungle, papaya also provides steady feasting for such mammals as kinkajous, coatimundis, monkeys and bats, as well as parrots, toucans and other birds.

a family of birds that eat nothing but insects scared up by marauding parties of army ants, yet manage to avoid the ants themselves.

Not only are living things more diverse in the tropics, but the relationships between them are more intricate. This complex interaction is exemplified in a genus of tree called ant acacia, common in the forests along the Pacific coast. Ant acacias have feathery leaves and branches that bear pairs of wicked inch-long thorns, rather like the horns of a fighting bull. Within the bases of the thorns dwell small but aggressive ants. The ants are attracted to the acacia by the presence of tiny nectaries—glands on the leaf stems that exude sugar—and by swellings on the leaf tips that are filled with proteins, lipides and vitamins. The adult ants eat the nectar and feed the swellings to their larvae. Clearly the ants gain a great deal from this arrangement. What the acacia gets out of it is less obvious, but no less satisfying.

The acacia goes to so much trouble to provide food and shelter for the ants in order to "hire" them as bodyguards. Though sun loving, the tree is a poor competitor in the race for sunlight; it is easily overshadowed by faster-growing neighbors. Nor do the acacia's leaves contain the toxic compounds that protect many tropical plants against predators. Weak and defenseless itself, the acacia needs some muscle, and the belligerent ants fill this function admirably. They defend their home tree fiercely against all comers. They attack any predator, from a cow to a leaf-eating insect, that touches the acacia. If a vine threatens to envelop the acacia, the ants cut the vine down. If the branch of a neighboring plant stretches too close, robbing the acacia of sunlight, the ants prune the interloper back. If the seeds of other plants fall on the ground beneath the acacia, the ants carry them away before they can germinate.

This relationship, in which both partners work actively on behalf of the corporation, is called mutualism. Rare in the temperate zones, it is relatively common in the competitive tropics, where the slightest advantage can make the difference between survival and extinction.

Among the legions of specialized creatures in the Central American jungles are the trogons, a family of insectivorous birds with unique skills. Temperate-zone insect-eating birds like flycatchers and warblers are almost frenetically active as they flit about in pursuit of their small, fast-moving prey. Tropical forests, though, contain not only small, busy insects, but many that are large, slow moving and well camouflaged. They represent a food resource that cannot be allowed to go to waste.

Trogons exploit this rich resource with a specialized "sit and wait" hunting technique. A trogon may perch on a branch for half an hour or an hour, moving only its head as it scans the forest with its sharp eyes. When a six-inch praying mantis or a big walking stick so much as moves a leg, the trogon flashes in for the kill. It very rarely misses.

Of all the trogon family, the most famous and spectacular member is the quetzal, the bird Jesús Flores and I were seeking in the cloud forest of Atitlán. The quetzal is so stunning that the ancient Maya incorporated its elegant form into their arts and crafts and used its feathers to adorn the costumes of their emperors. The Aztecs of Mexico pictured their main god wearing a crown of quetzal feathers; they called him, in fact, Quetzalcóatl, which means plumed serpent. They also imposed a death sentence on any commoner who killed a quetzal. Even today the monetary unit of Guatemala is called the quetzal. Many people consider the quetzal the most beautiful of all the world's birds, and bird watchers and naturalists come from all over the world to try to see it. But only the lucky are rewarded with a sighting; the quetzal has grown increasingly rare throughout Central America as its cloud-forest habitat has been encroached upon by cultivated fields.

Hoping for our own glimpse of the bird, Jesús and I continued to climb for about two hours on the slopes of the volcano. As we moved higher, the forest grew even more luxuriant, the tree limbs bearing heavier and heavier burdens of epiphytic plants until each branch was an aerial garden in itself. Philodendrons with leaves a foot across spiraled up the trunks; wrist-thick lianas dropped 100 feet from the canopy to the ground. The morning chorus of the *guardabarrancas* had ended, and the forest was silent except for the sound of our footsteps.

Finally we reached the lower levels of the clouds, and although the mist did not penetrate beneath the canopy, I could feel the dampness coming through my clothes. The mountain gets about 160 inches or more of rain a year, and even on a comparatively dry day such as this one the forest was able to produce its own internal rain, as evaporating moisture condensed on the cool leaves and fell to earth in droplets.

Ahead of me, Jesús paused and motioned for me to be silent. Then he continued on, with deliberate, slow-motion movements like those of a Chinese boxer, occasionally freezing in place with one foot suspended in mid-air. I followed as quietly as I could. After a few yards Jesús paused again and pointed at the trunk of a large dead tree that stood about 50 feet away on the steep side of a narrow ravine. *"Nido,"* he said. The nest. Thirty feet up the tree was a round hole perhaps four inches in diameter. It was probably an old woodpecker hole, and Jesús knew that recently a pair of quetzals had been enlarging it preparatory to raising their brood. We crouched behind a screen of vines, and Jesús began to call very softly, in a mournful two-note whistle.

Looking up, I could see coils of mist sliding through the treetops above us. It was chilly there at the level of the clouds, and I shivered a bit. After a while came a sound similar to the one Jesús had made, but so faint it was barely audible. Jesús called again. We listened, ears straining against the silence. Suddenly Jesús reached out and grabbed my wrist. "*Viene,*" he whispered hoarsely. It comes. We waited, not daring to move, for what seemed a very long time. And then the bird was there. I never saw it arrive, never saw the motion of wings, but suddenly I could sense something different about the greenness across the little ravine. I lifted the glasses, and there the bird was.

All of the photographs and paintings I had seen had not prepared me for the creature that appeared in the circle of my binoculars. It was green, but not any ordinary green. Its iridescent plumage seemed to vibrate in the soft light, as if the color itself were alive. When the bird shifted its position slightly on the branch, the green turned to blue, then glittered like gold as the light leaped from the plumage. The breast was a vibrant scarlet—the badge of a male. The tail, three feet long, swept down from the branch in a graceful arc.

The quetzal sat immobile, observing the jungle from a round, dark eye. The bird was so splendid that I held my breath for fear of frightening it away. But as I shifted slightly for a better view, a twig cracked under my knees. In the circle of my binoculars the quetzal became a whirl of brilliant feathers, a throb of color. And then it was gone.

NATURE WALK / Down the Slopes of Pacaya

Dawn was still several hours away when I set out with photographer Co Rentmeester to climb a ridge on the lower slopes of 8,373-foot Volcán Pacaya, one of Guatemala's active volcanoes. In the dark, the 1,000-foot ascent from the lowlands was difficult and tiring, but we wanted to reach the crest of the ridge in time to watch the sunrise on Pacaya's three neighboring volcanoes. Afterward, we proposed to spend the day working our leisurely way down the ridge again, so as to be back in the valley by evening. There at a small lake we hoped to see the arrival of huge flocks of cattle egrets, returning to roost after feeding all day nearby.

Pacaya rises from countryside that has broad areas under cultivation. But the land we were on, part of a sugar-cane plantation, had been left in a natural state by its owner, an active conservationist.

We reached the crest of the ridge about two hours after setting out; the stars were still bright in the clear sky. As we sat catching our breath, we could hear Pacaya's guttural roaring above us. We were at least 7,000 feet below the summit; but, sitting on the ground, it seemed to me I could feel tremors of eruption being transmitted up through the earth.

Within a few minutes the sky began to lighten. Then, very quickly, dawn came, the first alpenglow tinting the three large volcanoes that lay to our north. A cloud of volcanic ash streamed from the 12,655-foot summit of Fuego. Behind it stood 12,992-foot Acatenango, and just to the right the perfectly formed cone of the 12,337-foot Volcán de Agua, "the water volcano," which was named for the deluge of mud that poured down the mountain's flanks on September 10, 1541, obliterating Ciudad Vieja, Guatemala's ancient capital.

From our vantage point we had a fine view of the surrounding country, for it was November, and many of the trees were bare of leaves. Unlike the always-wet Caribbean slopes, here on the west side of Central America's mountain spine there is a distinct dry season, roughly corresponding on the calendar to winter in temperate zones to the north, except that the weather gets hotter rather than colder. For months on end very little rain falls and the trees husband water by shedding their leaves, which otherwise would dissipate vital moisture through transpiration. But while the trees were beginning to look spare, many smaller plants, coming to the end of their wet-season growth, were flowering.

All around us the eupatorium was blooming. Like the sunflower and the dandelion, it is a composite plant, whose showy blossoms are made up of scores of tiny white flowers. Twisted among the trees atop the ridge were calopogonium vines, their seed pods already beginning to mature. Both the pods and leaves of these common vines were covered with hairs, which probably serve, as they do in other plants, both to protect the vine from insects and to block winds that would desiccate it.

The sun was well up by the time we began to make our descent from the ridge crest along a crude trail that some cane cutters had slashed with their machetes. We passed a number of spiky-looking frangipani trees, now not only leafless but bare of the large and fragrant white blossoms for which they are famous—the flowers that the women of Tahiti

PACAYA'S VOLCANIC NEIGHBORS BEYOND A STAND OF EUPATORIUM

SEED PODS OF CALOPOGONIUM

LEAFLESS FRANGIPANI TREES

and Bali entwine in their hair. In spite of its association with the Pacific, the frangipani is also native here in the western-slope forests of Central America. And for all the delicacy of its flowers, the tree is able to endure heat and drought and to defend itself against insect and animal pests by producing a rubbery, poisonous sap that oozes out whenever its bark is punctured.

As we walked, the openness of the forest at this time of year made the birds easier to see. Shortly we came upon a turkey vulture perched on a bough, spreading its wings in the sun to dry away the morning dew. The turkey vulture is a frequent visitor in the forest, where its keen sense of smell helps it find carcasses to feed on even when it cannot spot them through the leaves.

To feel well disposed toward turkey vultures requires an effort of will. Yet they perform a useful function as recyclers of rotting flesh. Because of their naked heads and necks, they can feed on dead animals without getting their feathers matted with blood and offal. Sometimes they gorge themselves so full they cannot fly until they have regurgitated part of their meal.

On the ground turkey vultures lurch about in an ungainly waddle, but once in the air they soar with consummate skill, barely moving a feather for hour after hour. For soaring they rely on the lifting power of thermals, columns of warm air that rise from the heated earth; thus, in the cool of morning they find flight laborious and tend to take it easy,

A TURKEY VULTURE DRYING ITS WINGS

A FRUITING URERA PLANT

as the bird before us was doing.

A little farther down the trail I noticed a urera plant, a member of the nettle family, hung with ripe orange fruits that are favored by many birds. None were feeding here, however; evidently they had found good pickings elsewhere. As we paused, I swept my binoculars over some nearby trees and picked out a hummingbird no larger than my thumb, sitting in a demitasse-sized nest on a branch. After some fumbling in my field guide, I identified it by its very long bill and dull crown as a plain-capped starthroat and, with only a touch of red on the throat, a female. Since she didn't fly away, I suspected she was incubating her eggs.

Most birds of Central America breed at the start of the wet season. But on the Pacific slope, hummingbirds frequently nest in the winter. Since they feed primarily on nectar, they can take advantage of the rush

A PLAIN-CAPPED STARTHROAT

of blossoms the plants put forth in the sunny dry season.

A Cool Oasis

It was almost midday and growing hot when we reached the shaded pocket of a ravine notched into the ridge. The trees were taller here, and the canopy denser. The shade and shelter from the wind had trapped moisture, and the ground sprouted a richness of plant life.

Beside our path stood a huge boulder, perhaps 15 feet high and 30 feet long. On closer inspection, I saw that it was not a single boulder at all, but a kind of giant conglomerate, a group of good-sized rounded rocks embedded in a stony matrix. Later, when I described the boulder to a geologist, he informed me that it was a piece of volcanic vomitus, an agglomerate containing ash, cinders and other debris cemented together along with the big round rocks known as bombs—chunks of congealed magma

—that Pacaya had coughed up in some eruption long ago.

The boulder was encrusted with a number of epiphytic plants that elsewhere grow high in the branches of trees. There were bromeliads, which simply use the rock as a support and collect water and nutrients from the air in their cuplike clusters of leaves; and there were also aroids, which send stringy roots down the face of the rock to reach the soil.

In among the aroids were some monstera—large, showy plants resembling philodendrons, with two-foot-long, deeply notched leaves. I had often wondered why certain plants have such serrations, and it now occurred to me that perhaps they prevent big leaves from tearing when the wind gets at them. In any case the leaves were very handsome. Indeed, monstera has proved to be a popular house plant; accustomed to the deep shade of tropical forests, it also dwells happily indoors.

Since the ravine was relatively cool, we decided to rest there and eat our lunch. I took care to strip off my nylon rain jacket and put it on a log before sitting down, to forestall any biting insects that might find me tempting. While munching on the tortillas we had brought with us, I saw something flickering through the forest a little farther down the ravine. Before I could even focus my eyes, whatever it was had vanished. But I kept scanning the area where I had seen the movement and finally caught sight of a large owl butterfly with a five-inch wing span. In flight this butterfly is quite conspicuous,

RED-FLOWERED APHELANDRA AND AROID VINES BESIDE A VOLCANIC BOULDER

but is virtually impossible to detect the moment it drops to a perch and folds its wings.

An Insect Mimic

I was able to locate this specimen only because of the spots on the wings—which resemble the eyes of some big and fearsome owl, and thus frighten possible predators away. Although this butterfly had been flying at midday, normally members of the species sit quietly until dusk, when they begin to flit about the forest in search of the rotting fruits that they feed upon.

When we resumed our walk, we saw numerous signs of the labors of leaf-cutting ants, though the insects themselves were not to be seen. The delicate petals of a white-blossomed begonia had been spared but the leaves were riddled with holes. The ants had cut out sections of leaf and carried them back to a nest that might have been half a mile away.

Near the riddled begonia were some victuals quite suitable for human consumption: the fruits of wild papaya, hanging from a thick, now-leafless stem. Unfortunately for us, these were unripe; at maturity the pinkish-orange flesh is very tasty. And birds and small mammals prize the seeds so much that they rip away the papaya's skin to get at them.

In the moist habitat of the ravine we expected to encounter some frogs, and we did. One of them, a dark, warty little fellow, was so well camouflaged as to be almost invisible against the branch on which he sat. This frog rarely grows to more than an inch, has a name longer than its body—eleutherodactylus—and is

AN OWL BUTTERFLY

AN ANT-RAVAGED BEGONIA

A MONSTERA PLANT

WILD PAPAYA FRUITS

AN ELEUTHERODACTYLUS FROG

A HARVESTMAN ON A MORNING-GLORY

A TREE FROG *ATOP A HELICONIA LEAF*

quite common in Central America. Unlike many other rain-forest frogs, it generally lives on the ground and lays its eggs not in water but in the moist cups of leaves or in plant debris. I wondered how this habit affected the tadpoles, which naturally need water to survive.

I subsequently learned that eleutherodactylus goes through its tadpole stage inside the egg sac. When the tadpole hatches out, with the aid of a tiny egg tooth on the end of its snout, it is a perfect replica of the adult, but small enough to sit—along with a dozen others—on a man's fingernail. As minuscule as they are, the young frogs have far fewer enemies on the land than do tadpoles in the predator-filled pond waters. Thus the eleutherodactylus lays only a few dozen eggs, rather than the thousands produced by most frogs.

A Tree-Climbing Frog

Not far away we came upon a second frog, perched on a leaf a few feet above the ground. This was a hyla, a tree frog. With the enlarged suction-cup pads on their toes, hylas can climb virtually any surface, including vertical ones, and they spend their entire lives up in the foliage, usually descending to the ground only when seeking water in which to lay their eggs.

As we emerged from the ravine into a marshy area, we came to a small clearing thickly grown with wild morning-glory vines. The blossoms were profuse though fragile; each individual blossom lasts only for a day or two, which the plant makes up for by putting forth a great

many flowers over a long season.

On one of the blossoms rested a leggy little creature called a harvestman. In the United States we know its relative as the daddy longlegs, which many people think is a spider. They are not spiders, however, nor are they insects, but eight-legged arthropods, or segmented invertebrates, in a class by themselves. Perfectly harmless, they scavenge for dead insects or eat soft fruit. And, as any school child knows, they tickle if they walk on your arm.

We were at the foot of the ridge by now, and after a bit we reached a shallow pond, every inch of it covered by water lettuce. This plant floats on the surface, sending down roots that draw nutrients from the water itself and shooting out long runners on which new plants form. A single rosette of water lettuce can multiply so rapidly that it could completely blanket a small pond within a matter of months. Yet it is generally not a serious pest—as water hyacinth has become in the southern United States—for it requires still water and does not do well on streams or lakes of any size.

Toward evening Co and I reached our final destination—the small lake that lay near the foot of the ridge. As the sun skimmed across the treetops, the first egrets began to appear, slanting in low over the forest to their roosts in a big dead tree on the opposite shore. This was not a nesting site—the season was wrong—but rather a kind of giant avian motel, a stopover used as long as there was good feeding nearby.

A MAT OF WATER LETTUCE ON A JUNGLE POND

All the birds that roost here are cattle egrets, a species that frequently perches on the backs of grazing cattle. This egret is slightly smaller than its famous cousin, the snowy egret; nor does it have the snowy's elegant plumage. But it has been extraordinarily successful in recent times. Native to Africa, cattle egrets reached South America by some unknown means around 1930. Since then they have increased their numbers and expanded their range. Today the cattle egret is found as far north as Newfoundland.

Unlike the African oxpecker and other birds that have worked out symbiotic relationships with large herbivores, these birds do not pick parasites from their cattle hosts. Instead, they eat insects, frogs and other small creatures stirred up in the course of the animals' passage through the grass.

As the light of day began to yellow with sunset, we watched more and more birds come streaming in. Flocks of 10 now became flocks of 50 or 100. Each arrival produced a flurry of flapping and squawking as the newcomers tried to find places for themselves on the crowded branches. No sooner did the occupants of the tree quiet down than another flock arrived, throwing the roost into an uproar again. But just as the sunset faded into dusk, the incoming flights slowed to a trickle; the egrets settled themselves for the night, and the roost bloomed like a great white flower on the shore of the little lake.

CATTLE EGRETS ROOSTING

BROAD-LEAFED FOREST AROUND THE EGRETS' LAKESIDE SHELTER

2/ The Land Formed by Fire

*In all the terrifying phenomena attending eruptions
—earthquakes, floods, showers of ashes, thunder and
lightning—there is a certain majestic beauty, though a beauty
that is savage and untamed.*   CHRISTOPH KRÜGER/ *VOLCANOES*

From the Pacific coast of Central America one is always in sight of volcanoes. Their great cones and domes dominate the landscape from 13,812-foot Tajumulco in Guatemala to 11,410-foot Barú in Panama. The people of Central America have held these volcanoes in awe for centuries, and their fear is recorded in the earth in the middle of Nicaragua's capital, Managua. While quarrying there in the 1880s workmen found, frozen in hardened mud a few feet below the surface, several sets of human footprints. Scientists summoned to the site concluded that the tracks had been preserved in the mud and ash spewed forth during an eruption of Volcán Masaya, 15 miles away. At first the tracks were thought to have been made by people living between 50,000 and 200,000 years ago. More recent investigations have shown them to be about 10,000 years old.

A shelter was built over the tracks to protect them from erosion, and they survive today as a testimonial to the panic of primitive people fleeing from what must have seemed the end of the world. In the patch of exposed mud, now turned solid as rock, are the prints of half a dozen people, all heading away from the volcano toward nearby Lake Managua. Mixed in with the human tracks are prints of a deer, a cat and other animals, all perfectly recognizable after several thousand years.

The human prints are widely spaced, as if the people were running as fast as they could through the glutinous mud. There are the large tracks of a man, the tiny tracks of a child, the medium-sized tracks of a woman or youth. One set is punched in more than 12 inches deep for several strides; then suddenly the prints become shallow and the strides lengthen. Presumably someone had been carrying a heavy burden, perhaps a bundle of possessions, and had then, as the hot ash and fiery coals rained from the sky, thrown off the load to run for his life.

It is still possible to share the emotions of those early people, for today Central America is one of the world's most restless volcanic centers. The geologic forces that originally created the isthmus are still at work. The Cocos Plate—which caused the volcanoes to be thrust up as it moved eastward from the Pacific and began to push against the Caribbean Plate—continues on the move.

Central America has 36 active volcanoes and 43 that are dormant but still capable of eruption. In Guatemala alone there are eight active volcanoes, and at any given moment two or three are apt to be noticeably alive. At dusk, from the highway just outside Guatemala City, glowing rivers of lava can be seen pouring down the flanks of Pacaya 24 miles to the south; up until a few years ago, one could observe plumes of volcanic ash belching from Fuego 27 miles to the southwest. As recently as 1974 Fuego spewed forth so much ash that it inundated villages on its slopes. For months afterward, people in the Northern Hemisphere were treated to spectacular sunsets—the result of the sun's rays being refracted through a layer of volcanic dust from Fuego, circling the earth at an altitude of 10 to 12 miles.

In spite of the threat of such outbursts, the Guatemalans, like other Central Americans, continue to live hard by their volcanoes. The lava-based soil is so rich in nutrients that the volcanic flanks are prime agricultural land; high on the slopes of Picaya, for example, farmers work their crops even as lava courses down less than a mile away and the roar of eruption splits the air.

Nicaragua has 10 volcanoes, one of which, Cosigüina, was responsible for the greatest explosion in the history of Latin America. In 1835, with a bang unequaled by the biggest H-bomb ever detonated, Cosigüina blasted into the air as much as six cubic miles of debris—a quantity so enormous that had it settled on the ground it would have blanketed about 30,000 square miles with a foot-deep layer. An Englishman who was staying some 60 miles from Cosigüina reported: "To add to the terror of the day, at intervals smart shocks of earthquake made themselves felt, and a distant roaring, like thunder afar off, was heard . . . still the ashes fell; and so passed that day, the very birds entering into the rooms where candles were burning, but scarcely visible."

I went to visit one of Nicaragua's volcanoes, guided by Dr. Jaime Incer of the University of Central America. Dr. Incer is a biologist with an all-encompassing interest in the natural world. As we drove south from Managua in his Jeep, he talked enthusiastically about the volcanic activity of the region. "The city of Managua is built on layer upon layer of old volcanic mud flows, ash, cinders and pumice—which is really just hardened volcanic foam," he said. "I wouldn't be surprised," he added, "if a volcano appeared tomorrow in my own backyard." I had the feeling that if one did, Dr. Incer would be delighted.

About a dozen miles outside of Managua we turned off onto a rough track through 200-year-old lava flows. They were partially overgrown by vegetation that was helping to transform the sharp-edged, clinker-like volcanic rock into soil. The lava was dotted with lichens and mosses and small ferns. Cactus and white-blossomed frangipani thrust up from the rocks. Tiny orchids grew from chinks, taking advantage of the nutrients in the organic litter that had already been deposited by other plants.

After a while we reached the crown of Volcán Masaya. The original top had collapsed long ago, leaving an enormous depression, or caldera, some seven miles across. Within this depression eight vents appeared, the largest one named Santiago. It was toward Santiago, the most active vent in recent years, that we now headed. We left the car and walked to the edge of a crater about 750 feet deep and more than twice that across. Below its sheer walls lay a bed of hard, blackened lava. In the center of this old lava a well-like shaft dropped another 50 feet or so to a pool of molten lava that was sloshing to and fro. At a temperature of about 1,300° F. the incandescent rock looked as liquid as water, and surged like surf against the walls of the shaft.

We stood there, watching, for a long time. Pungent fumes drifted over us, stinging our noses with the sharp smell of chlorine and sulfur dioxide. From time to time the lava in the shaft spurted up in great gouts; each time, after a few seconds, we would hear an explosive crack, like the sound of distant artillery. Brilliant-green little parakeets flew about within the crater; somehow these birds tolerate the fumes and the uproar, nesting in chinks in the crater walls.

Santiago has been in more or less continuous turmoil ever since the first Europeans reached Central America, and as we stood on the rim, Dr. Incer told me something of the crater's history. In 1538 a Spanish

On the steep slope of Santiago, one of eight huge craters that pit Volcán Masaya in Nicaragua, layers of rust-colored basalt intermingle with whitish ash—the products of successive eruptions. The fiery hot magma in the vent in the foreground gives evidence of Santiago's continuing unrest.

monk visited the crater, concluded that the bright-red stuff in the bottom was molten gold, and tried to enrich himself by scooping some out with a pot attached to a long chain; he became disillusioned when the pot melted. Later, other monks sent sinners to the edge of the crater for a glimpse of what was thought to be the mouth of hell—a penance guaranteed to make backsliders correct their ways.

After a major eruption in 1924, fumes from Santiago devastated coffee crops on the slopes of the nearby mountains. Two German engineers devised a scheme to cap Santiago's vent; after a year and a half of work with high explosives, they had almost succeeded in collapsing the crater and closing the vent when Santiago erupted anew. It blew its lid again 19 years later, and once more clouds of poisonous vapor destroyed the coffee crops. The coffee growers then came up with a variety of bizarre solutions for their volcanic problem. One plan called for constructing a 1,000-foot chimney to carry the fumes away; someone suggested dropping an atomic bomb into the crater to collapse it. In 1953 the Nicaraguan Air Force did, in fact, launch a raid on Santiago. Planes dropped two medium-sized conventional bombs—to no effect.

Within the last few years Santiago has not been spouting its noxious gases in such destructive quantities. "But," Dr. Incer reminded me, "who knows what will happen tomorrow?"

Nobody. And for Nicaraguans there is another constant natural threat associated with the volcanoes and in many ways more dire—earthquake. For this, too, the Cocos Plate is responsible. In its travels eastward, stresses broke it into seven segments, which moved forward at somewhat different depths and different angles. The breaks, or faults, that lie between the segments provide a means through which subterranean energies can find escape in the form of earthquakes.

By an accident of history, Nicaragua's capital of Managua was settled atop one of the faults—in a geological sense, probably the worst imaginable site for a city. In the late 19th Century Managua was shaken by a severe quake and in 1931 it was partially destroyed by another. Then, on December 23, 1972, the earth moved once more. Within an hour three quakes destroyed most of central Managua and took some 11,000 lives. Today, the core of the city—six square miles—is an open area of green parks and sports fields, where few buildings remain.

Walking through the center of Managua, or looking down from the rim of Santiago at the waves of lava, I found it easy to feel the sense of apocalypse that Nicaraguans have always lived with. It was easy, too, to comprehend that nature remains large and man small; that the earth is a pulsing ball of powerful energies demanding continual release.

Were it not for the volcanoes and earthquakes, the transisthmian canal would probably have been built in Nicaragua rather than in Panama. For Nicaragua contains a fresh-water lake so immense that it almost links the two oceans. Forty-five miles wide and over 100 miles long, Lake Nicaragua is the largest body of fresh water in the Americas between the Great Lakes and Lake Titicaca. Under strong winds the water is apt to rise and fall several feet at certain points along the shore; early Spaniards therefore believed the lake had tides, and indeed named it El Mar Dulce, "The Sweet Sea."

The lake, along with its smaller neighbor, Lake Managua, drains into the Caribbean down the 117-mile-long course of the Río San Juan. But despite this direct connection with the Caribbean, Lake Nicaragua really lies much closer to the Pacific; indeed, at one point the distance from the lake shore to the Pacific is only 12 miles. Thus separated from one ocean only by a narrow strip of land and joined to the other by a large river, the lake offers a direct line of transport and communication from sea to sea. The struggle to dominate this line brought Nicaragua centuries of tragedy and strife—occupation, civil war and successive invasions by pirates, soldiers of fortune and imperialist freebooters.

By the late 19th Century, the idea for a Nicaraguan canal had influential backing in the United States. But in 1902, after Mont Pelée erupted in Martinique and killed 30,000 people, the United States became acutely volcano-conscious. An enterprising promoter of the Panama route dug up a Nicaraguan stamp bearing the picture of a volcano and sent one to each member of Congress as a reminder that a Nicaraguan canal would forever be menaced by geologic catastrophe. Congress soon authorized construction of a canal in Panama.

Though abandoned as a potential international trade artery, Lake Nicaragua has remained an object of fascination for scientists and other observers curious about natural phenomena. For while the waters of the lake are fresh, they are inhabited by several species of fish usually associated with salt water—the tarpon, the sawfish and the bull shark. That in itself is not surprising; all three are classified as euryhaline species—that is, they can and do cross from salt water into fresh and back again with no ill effects. In Florida, tarpon range far up into coastal estuaries and river mouths; the bull shark has turned up in Iquitos, Peru, 2,100 miles up the Amazon from its mouth.

The thing that intrigued ichthyological observers of Lake Nicaragua was not that the fish were there, but how they got there. All three species appeared to be totally landlocked, cut off from the Pacific by a ridge of land and from the Caribbean by rapids in the Río San Juan. One possible explanation lay in a long-standing theory that the lake was originally an arm of the Pacific, a giant bay, which was eventually cut off from the ocean by the upthrusting of Nicaragua's coastal volcanoes. An obvious corollary would be that the fish lived in the lake while it was still a part of the Pacific, were trapped by the uplifting of the land and settled down to a new life as fresh-water fish. This was precisely what early ichthyologists did believe. But they failed to take one factor into account—the tarpon existed only in the Atlantic. How could it possibly have reached the lake from the Pacific side?

The answer was not quickly forthcoming, even from revised and modernized ideas of the geologic origins of the lake. Studies made in the early 1960s showed that there were no marine sediments on the lake bottom, and thus the lake could never have been part of the Pacific —or the Atlantic either. Probably it had been formed by movements of the earth's crust along fault lines. And in fact later investigation proved that a pair of fault lines had developed some time ago along what are now the approximate boundaries of Lake Nicaragua and Lake Managua. The huge block of land between the faults slipped downward; the resulting depression, sometimes called the Great Rift, gradually filled with water, and the lakes that formed drained to the Caribbean down the trench of the San Juan.

The basic ichthyological puzzle remained. How did the fish get to Lake Nicaragua in the first place? A new line of inquiry revealed that back in the 16th Century ships of up to 120 tons were navigating the San Juan all the way from the Caribbean to the lake. Indeed, pirates periodically sailed up the river to loot and burn the lakeside settlements. But sometime in the middle of the next century, the speculation went, a series of violent earthquakes created rapids that not only made navigation more difficult but also barred access upstream to the fish. Thus a new theory emerged that the fish had freely entered the lake until the mid-17th Century and had been landlocked ever since.

A detailed analysis of the lake shark's morphology turned up evidence that all previous theories had been in error. For the sharks in the lake, assumed until then to have evolved into a fresh-water species, turned out to be identical to their salt-water counterparts. Ichthyologists now began to tag sharks both in the lake and in the Caribbean, affixing to some of them devices that emitted an ultrasonic pulse detectable by onshore receivers. Before long, three sharks tagged in the sea off Costa Rica were discovered in Lake Nicaragua. Nine sharks tagged in the lake were found in the Caribbean near the mouth of the San Juan. The mystery was solved: the sharks, and presumably the tarpon and sawfish, moved back and forth between lake and sea, breasting rapids previously thought impassable for these species.

Hoping for a look at these aquatic commuters, I went out on the lake one day with a fisherman named Luis Largusa and his young brother. Early in the morning we left the lakeside city of Granada in Luis' boat. He called his craft a *lancha,* a launch, but it was really only a big canoe, built of planks on the long, narrow lines of a dugout, and powered by a rust-covered seven-horse outboard that barely moved us through the water. As we came out of the wind-shadow of the land and entered the open water, a wave smashed over the bow, drenching me, shocking me with cold. We dropped into the trough and I saw a bigger wave coming, mounded above the horizon. I turned and looked back at Luis. His brown face was wet, and the wave had soaked the Sunday-best clothes that I suspected he was wearing in honor of his gringo passenger. *"Muy bravo,"* he said. Very rough. He grinned. I didn't grin back.

As we came farther out of the lee of land the waves grew larger and more menacing. Sometimes they smashed over the bow or the gunwales, and from behind me I could hear the sound of Luis' brother bailing rapidly with a can. Ahead of us, far down the lake, the twin volcanic cones on the island of Ometepe tilted erratically back and forth as we humped over the swells. Luis' nets, set out the day before, were three and a half uncomfortable hours away, and Luis could never tell in advance whether the long trip would be worthwhile. If he were very lucky he would find a sawfish in the nets, for to those who fish for a livelihood it is the most important creature in the lake.

Sawfish are really rays, structurally much like mantas or sting rays. They bear live young, which are perfect replicas of the parents except that—fortunately for the mother—the saw teeth on a baby's bill are covered by a membrane. The bill soon becomes a formidable weapon with which the sawfish stuns or impales the small fish it preys upon. In the ocean, sawfish reach a length of 20 feet, with bills as long as four feet. Even in the lake they weigh up to 750 pounds, and their flesh, cut into fish sticks and frozen, fetches a good price on the international market.

The lake sharks are also big fish, weighing up to 200 pounds, but because of a peculiar quirk of their physiology their flesh is usually inedible. In most fish, the urea formed from bodily wastes is passed out of the body as quickly as it is produced; sharks, however, retain large quantities of urea in the bloodstream. Thus, if a shark is not bled and cleaned immediately after death, the meat spoils very rapidly.

A fisherman keeps a shark's flesh only if he finds one fresh caught and still alive in the nets—a circumstance that, according to Luis, can be quite dangerous. The sharks are impressively armed with multiple rows of teeth; they struggle violently, and they are hard to kill. Regarded as offensive creatures wherever they live, bull sharks in Lake Nicaragua have earned a reputation as particularly nasty customers. Ephraim Squier, the first United States minister in Nicaragua, wrote in 1852 that the sharks had "killed bathers within a stone's throw of the beach at Granada, and I have myself seen them from the walls of the old castle, dashing about, with their fins projecting above the water." Attacks on human beings are still reported from time to time.

For hours Luis' little boat climbed slowly over the backs of the waves, heading toward the cones of Ometepe. From the tops of the waves, when I looked toward the lake's eastern shore, I could see no land at all, just a seemingly limitless expanse of water. Occasionally small terns, enviably buoyant and airborne, slid overhead in the gusting wind, their sharp beaks pointed straight down as they looked for prey.

Around noon, Luis spotted his net marker bobbing on the waves. He cut the engine and then he and his brother moved forward and began hauling up the quarter-mile-long gill net. After a few minutes I smelled a powerful stench, and looking ahead I saw what appeared to be a big white balloon enmeshed in the net. It was a garfish, its belly distended by internal gases, and in death its smell was so fierce I had to hold my breath while Luis cut it from the net and threw it back into the water.

Another 100 yards of net and another fish appeared. Dead, it was still a beautiful thing to look at. It was a tarpon of about 50 pounds, its sides covered with huge scales as bright as freshly minted silver dollars. Even its eyes gleamed with a silvery iridescence. But Luis took a quick look into the gills to check their color, pronounced the fish dead too long and dropped it back into the lake. The tarpon shafted downward, a metallic gleam descending into the gray water.

I found that a sad thing to witness. These giant relatives of the herring are among the world's most magnificent game fish. When hooked they go berserk—they dive, run and leap from the water again and again, shaking their heads violently in attempts to throw the hook. A

Smallest of Atitlán's three volcanoes, 10,000-foot San Pedro has been dormant so long that corn is farmed more than halfway to the top.

Volcanoes in Varied Guises

Perhaps the most dramatic aspect of the Central American wilderness is the chain of 60 varied—and often violent—volcanoes along the Pacific coast. These lethal mountains differ not only in the way they behave but also in the form they take. Some, like Guatemala's Volcán Pacaya (right), have the look classically associated with volcanoes—a graceful cone shape topped by a single crater from which lava spews sporadically. Others sprawl untidily, their summits swallowed by a huge depression, known as a caldera, which may be miles wide and scarred by steaming, smoking crevices. Still others are scalloped by several craters, dormant so long that lush green growth clothes their slopes.

Changes in a volcano's terrain result from many different causes. In the quieter volcanoes, at least part of the transformation comes about through weathering and erosion. In active mountains, the kind of change that takes place is dictated mainly by the nature of the eruption.

The essential ingredient of volcanic activity is magma—molten, gas-charged rock that rises after it has been liquefied by subterranean heat and friction. But not all magma is the same consistency. Some oozes steadily upward as a fiery soup of lava that eventually spurts up over the edges of a mountain such as Pacaya. Paradoxically, such frequent and relatively minor releases of power reduce the chances of a catastrophic blowup—and of a radical revision in shape.

The type of magma that fuels most Central American volcanoes, however, is thick, viscous, and so filled with gases that the erupting magma often blasts violently into the air. If it emerges in great quantity, it may leave a void into which the volcano's entire top falls, turning the summit into a caldera. That happened to Costa Rica's Irazú (pages 62-63), within whose wide-yawning gap three craters and three volcanic cones have formed.

Poás (pages 64-71), also in Costa Rica, reacted to eruption in its own way, venting its energies through three separate craters. Two now slumber under a blanket of vegetation; one even cradles a lake. But the third crater bubbles persistently, a visible manifestation of underground forces straining for release.

A pillar of fire issues from the heart of Pacaya while lava streams down the flanks of a cone newly formed at the mountain's old summit. One of Central America's most active volcanoes, Pacaya lies in Guatemala's most populous area. But its outbursts are rarely lethal, being limited to minor lava flows, fumes and occasional chunks of congealed magma—called bombs—that are blown out of the cone and bounce down the mountainside.

Mountains That Collapse Inward

Wide-topped volcanoes like Irazú (left) have a fearsome look because of the sheer size of the cavity at the summit. Such a mammoth basin, or caldera—from the Spanish word for caldron—may measure as much as 10 miles in diameter; a conventional crater, by contrast, is no more than a mile across.

A caldera was once thought to be the result of an eruption that sheared off the mountaintop. In fact, it is formed when the sudden evacuation of great masses of magma creates a vast empty space into which the volcanic cone topples. The monumental collapse may snuff out volcanic activity for a while, but not necessarily for all time.

Irazú's top fell in eons ago; then periodic small eruptions of lava and ash built up new cinder cones, like a set of nesting cups, within the ancient caldera. In 1963, when this picture was taken, Irazú broke a 20-year silence to begin disgorging great clouds of smoke and ash. The binge lasted for a period of two years, then abruptly ceased.

Irazú belches steam and dark volcanic ash during its 1963-1965 eruption. At one point, ash-filled water vapor blasted up into overhanging clouds and triggered a bizarre storm that rained mud, covering the surrounding area with a layer up to five inches thick.

A Spectacle of Three Craters

Costa Rica's Poás is a restless giant that measures some four miles across at its base. Its ridges rise almost 9,000 feet and enclose three separate, very large craters. All are so-called collapse craters—smaller than calderas but formed in the same way—and each has its own look. Two are dormant, their slopes now mantled by greenery; and one of these shelters a lake (pages 70-71).

The third crater (left) hints at the residual power of Poás. In 1910 magma forced its way through a large vent in the crater, sending up a column of steam and ash four miles high. In the 1950s Poás stirred again with a small eruption whose ash residue formed a new cone on the crater floor; the cone is now 200 feet high and still puffing.

Today a hellish landscape surrounds the cone. A field of ash, fallen from the slopes, lies barren and slicked by rain. A pool of steaming mud gives off water vapor and other gases. The crater's restive state has made Costa Ricans wary. Though Poás has been designated a national park, and has about 75,000 visitors each year, it is carefully monitored for signs of heightened activity.

Viewed from a ridge that was once part of the old volcanic cone, a recently formed cone (center) lies nested among terraced relics of past upheavals. The ash, pumice and lava layers at right are colored both by oxidation and by acidic emissions from the new cone.

The yellow stain of sulfur crystals
around a 12-inch-wide hole (above) in
Poás' active crater indicates that gases
periodically escape here, crystallizing
on contact with the air. The hole itself,
called a fumarole, is a tiny cousin of
the large outlet shown at left, and serves
as a vent for pent-up volcanic forces.

The liveliest sign of volcanic activity on
Poás is this 800-foot-wide pool of
steam-heated rain water mixed with
ash. The pool changes color from milky
white to jade green whenever a fresh
batch of sulfurous gas surges up from
the magma below, turning the hot
water into a solution of sulfuric acid.

Chunks of lava, washed from the upper rim of Poás by rain runoff, form a random pattern on the ash floor of the volcano's active crater.

Holes of unknown origin pit the surface of a small area of compacted ash (above). They may have been etched by acid-laden liquids rushing through the rock as it cooled during formation.

Frozen lava from an old eruption clings to a Poás slope (below). The bubbly, sand-castle look typifies quick-flowing lava that cools and begins to harden the instant that it leaves a vent.

This jungle-rimmed lake rests in one of Poás' placid craters. Wide-leafed gunnera, viburnum, amaryllis and other vegetation cloak the once-bleak crater walls. The walls themselves are of porous volcanic rock, rich in calcium and phosphorus, and weathered into fertile soil. Botanists believe that windborne seeds, nurtured by the soil and abundant rain, began to take hold as soon as the crater became dormant.

3/ An Unyielding Green Fortress

Buckled by the massive roots of even more massive trees . . . folded and creased by a million years of wear and tear, cluttered with vines and thorn trees, guarded by hornets and ants, it offered no easy access.

RUSSELL BRADDON/ *THE HUNDRED DAYS OF DARIEN*

The rain began before daybreak with a clap of thunder so loud that I woke and snapped upright on the cot. A few drops of water were already spattering against the screen walls. Then, within seconds, the rain descended on the roof with the force of a waterfall. I sat listening for a while; the noise made sleep impossible. Usually, by this hour, the howler monkeys had begun their morning chorus, and though they are not particularly aggressive as monkeys go, the reveille calls of the males sound like the battle cries of prehistoric carnivores. But on this morning, in the roar of the rain, I could not have heard the howlers even if they had been competing with the deluge.

I was in Panama, at a field research station of the Gorgas Memorial Laboratory, a center for the study of tropical diseases. The station is on the Río Bayano some 60 miles east of the canal. The Bayano was in the process of being dammed for a big hydroelectric project; back in Panama City I had heard a popular song, the lyrics of which ran: "El Projecto Bayano will solve the electrical crisis of Panama." Not long after my visit, the high ground on which the research station stood became an island preserve where the laboratory's scientists carry out their research in undisturbed jungle.

After about 20 minutes the rain slackened. Down toward the river the shapes of the trees began to show against the dawn sky. I dressed and sprayed myself with insect repellent, then had a quick breakfast in the cookshack. As I ate, the rain drummed dully on the thatch-palm roof and ran down the fronds into puddles on the ground. Above my head rats rustled in the thatch; soon Mr. Hinds, the station manager, would check his rodent traps, and if any rats had been caught during the night he would take blood samples from them and test them for the presence of encephalitis and other tropical diseases.

Full daylight came quickly, as it does in the tropics. The rain stopped; patches of blue appeared in the sky. I crammed my wide-brimmed hat down over my ears, stuck my rain parka and pants in my day pack, and started out on a trail into the forest. Mud sucked at my boots and I aimed my ritual curse at them. For my travels in Central America I had brought with me as basic footgear a pair of United States Army jungle boots, of the type designed for use in Vietnam. Though functional enough in the shin-deep water of Southeast Asia's paddies, the boots were an abomination in the lowlands of Central America. On trails that were always ribbons of mud, the drainage holes and fabric sides of the boots let more water in than out, and great gobs of the viscous mud clung to the lugged rubber soles.

I had gone just a short distance down the trail when the rain began again—not the fulminating downpour of the dawn, but hard and steady. I put on my parka and my rain pants and continued walking. After a couple of hundred yards I was soaking wet from the condensation of sweat inside the impermeable clothes. Many experienced jungle hands, I know, do not bother with rain gear at all; they prefer to get drenched with rain water rather than with their own perspiration. I stopped beneath a tree that gave me some shelter and unzipped my parka to let the steam and body heat escape. As I stood there, the rain came still harder, the jungle green fading to gray behind the barrier of water.

Rain is a fact of life in Central America, particularly on the Caribbean coast, on the flanks of its mountains and in the lowlands of Panama. Warm winds, with their great capacity for absorbing moisture, sweep in from the Atlantic and across the Caribbean. When they reach the Central American land mass the warm air is thrust upward; as it cools, the load of moisture it has gathered condenses into rain. From May to December, when the sun enhances the wind's moisture-carrying capacity, the Caribbean coast endures a six-month wet season in which the rainfall averages between 60 and 80 inches.

Sometimes the rain falls without letup for several days and nights on end. At other times, explosive thunderstorms and heavy overcasts alternate with periods when the sky is clear and the sopping jungle steams

A poisonous parrot snake, a variety of tree-dwelling viper, wends its sinuous way down through jungle branches.

under brilliant sunshine. In the wet season, 23 hours of a given day may be dry and pleasant; during the 24th, I sometimes wondered if I could survive without a life raft.

Slogging on again through the forest, I could see very few signs of wildlife. Mercifully, the rain ended after a while and the sun streamed down through the broken canopy above the trail. But despite the brightness, and though I stopped frequently to scan the trailside treetops, the monkeys that I knew were common in the area eluded me, and even the birds were silent. Occasionally I spotted a small lizard flicking away from the trail's edge; sometimes big morpho butterflies zigzagged across my path, their iridescent blue wings flashing like mirrors in the sun.

Then, rounding a bend in the trail, I saw what appeared to be a swarm of small green butterflies marching over the ground a few yards ahead of me. At a closer look they proved to be leaf-cutting ants, hundreds upon hundreds, in a column about three inches wide. Many of the ants carried upright in their jaws a circular green shard scissored from the leaves of a plant; each of these ants, with its outsize burden, looked like a sloop under heavy sail.

Fascinated, I squatted on my haunches, my boots only a few inches from the edge of the column, and watched for a long while. The column extended from the forest on one side of the trail into the undergrowth on the other. The path it followed was clean of debris, immaculate as a swept doorstep, and ants moved in both directions along it. Those moving from my left were unladen; those moving from my right were carrying the circular bits of leaf.

Somewhere to my right, in the forest, was a plant whose leaves were now neatly scalloped where the ants had cut away their booty. Somewhere off to my left was the ants' nest, a low mound of bare earth perhaps 15 feet across. It was once thought that the ants carried the leaves back to their nest in order to eat them, but the truth is more complicated. The ants are really mushroom farmers. At the nest they place the leaves in dark underground chambers; a fungus grows on the decaying leaves, and the ants eat the fungus.

Leaf cutters are so persistent in their labors that they drove some early naturalists to distraction. Henry Bates, the great naturalist of the Amazon, found that his supply of cassava meal, which he used to make bread, was being carried away by the ants grain by grain; they had discovered that the meal made a good substratum for their fungus farms. Bates finally had to incinerate the ant columns with gunpowder. In Nicaragua, the 19th Century naturalist Thomas Belt was frustrated again and again in his horticultural experiments; he no sooner planted a banana, mango or orange tree than the leaf cutters denuded it. Belt searched out the ant nest and plugged up all the entrance holes; the ants excavated new ones and headed straight back to Belt's garden. He then dug deep into the ant mound and destroyed the underground chambers; still the ants returned. Finally Belt poured carbolic acid into the nest holes, a stratagem that drove the leaf cutters away long enough for the experiments to be completed.

I had been told that the leaf cutters maintain their orderly line of march by exuding pheromones—hormone-like substances that release a scent easily recognized by other ants of the same species. As I watched the ants crossing my own path, I wondered what would happen if their scent trail was interrupted. Would they march off in all directions, never again to find their nest? Or would pioneer ants blaze a new trail? I decided to inconvenience the leaf cutters in the name of science. I took out my can of insect repellent and sprayed an eight-inch section of their trail. The effect was immediate. The leading ants stopped at the edge of the sprayed area and began milling about. As more and more ants reached the barrier, they were caught up in a preposterous miniature traffic jam. Some ants started marching purposefully back the way they had just come. Others dropped their loads and wandered around aimlessly. A few, still clutching their leaves, moved out to either side of the break and tried to pick up the trail again.

Finally one ant, still bearing its leaf, found a way around the edge of the sprayed patch and rejoined the trail on the other side. A few minutes later several more ants followed this tiny Daniel Boone and made it around the break. About 25 minutes after I had sprayed the column it was flowing smoothly again.

I tried another experiment, simply scraping my boot across the trail to scatter the scent. Again confusion ensued; but this time the ants bridged the gap in only 10 minutes. Deciding that I had harried the industrious leaf cutters enough by now, I left them and went on my way.

In Panama, the traveler begins to feel the presence of the South American continent. Panamanians, in fact, do not even consider themselves Central Americans; their historical and ecological ties have been to South America. The plants and creatures of the southern continent clearly dominate in Panama. Both its coasts are hot, wet and tropical, though very different in look; the Caribbean shore slopes down to a

A poison arrow frog, fully matured at one inch, crouches on a leaf in wait for passing insects. Though tiny, the frog is safe from virtually all predators. Glands in the frog's skin produce a poison so lethal it was once used by Panamanian Indians to tip their hunting arrows: a wounded animal would become paralyzed or die when the poison entered its bloodstream.

fringe of low-lying islands covered with coconut palms, while the Pacific coast is more dramatic, the land falling away abruptly into a deep blue sea. But anywhere on the isthmus there is always the prospect of seeing some bird or animal that also lives along the Amazon.

And in fact the animal I was most hoping to see along this stretch of trail was one whose ancestry is distinctly South American, and which is perhaps the strangest creature of the jungle canopy—the sloth. Sloth watching can be a supremely restful pastime, since sloths do nothing without long, careful deliberation. When they finally act, they move with the glacial speed of cold molasses. Indeed the sloth is so torpid that in some respects it seems more vegetable than animal. Its fur is overgrown by algae and inhabited by moths. Even its digestive processes are deliberate. Once a week the sloth descends to the base of its tree and defecates. That problem taken care of, the sloth returns to its treetop for another week of eating.

Since they are slow and homely, and have never been accused of possessing great intelligence, sloths did not always fare well at the hands of naturalists and others who encountered them in the early years of exploration. Oviedo y Valdés, a 16th Century Spanish knight who was one of the first chroniclers of Central America, wrote that he had never seen "an uglier animal, or appearing as useless as this one." Later, in a somewhat warped spirit of scientific inquiry, Captain William Dampier whipped a sloth to see if it would move faster—it did not. In 1748 a Spanish sea captain reported that the sloth was so lazy it dropped fruits to the ground, then curled itself into a ball and plummeted from its tree, in order to avoid the work of climbing down. "One more defect," wrote the French naturalist Buffon, "and it would cease to survive."

Despite the bad press the sloth has received over the centuries, it is very well adapted to its arboreal life. Its slow movements and algae-covered hair make it difficult for a predator to spot. Its habitual upside-down posture is ideal for feeding on drooping leaves and fruits. With its hooklike claws and careful movements, the sloth travels with great sureness and safety along its precarious highways in the forest canopy. (By contrast, agile monkeys sometimes take bad falls.) Neither of the two species of sloth in Central America is really aggressive, but while the three-toed sloth is a fairly placid animal, its two-toed cousin has a quick temper and leather-punch teeth that can splinter a one-inch board, and it can give a good account of itself in combat against ocelots and other enemies. Both species of sloth are extremely tough, capable of surviving wounds and traumatic shocks that would kill other creatures.

The sloth's most notable characteristic—its sloth—results from the fact that it has a low basal metabolism and a relatively small amount of muscle tissue compared to other animals of the same size. The two-toed sloth, the speedster of the pair, can hit a top speed of about three hours to the mile. The three-toed sloth would require about four and a half hours to cover a mile—about the same as a tortoise. Neither species can maneuver very well on the ground; both must drag themselves arduously along by grasping at roots or stems or irregularities in the earth. But since a sloth may pass its entire lifetime within a grove of perhaps 50 trees, suspended from one branch or another, its clumsiness on the ground is not so great a disadvantage as it might seem.

Aware of the sloth's limited radius, I kept my eyes peeled as I moved down the trail. But even the best-peeled eyes do not guarantee successful slothing, for the creature's camouflage makes it virtually invisible unless the observer has acquired a so-called search image—a biologist's term for the refined visual sensitivity that allows the eye to spot an animal however well concealed. Search images are gained only through long experience. A few weeks earlier, on Barro Colorado Island, I had gone for a walk with a Panamanian who had this gift. Within a short distance he stopped four times to point up to the canopy and pronounce: "Perezoso—lazy." Each time, it took me five minutes of scanning to spot the "lazy," as Panamanians describe the sloth, hanging like a blob of greenish-gray moss in the treetops.

I did, at last, see a sloth in the forest at Bayano, but in circumstances neither of us could enjoy. In the afternoon, I reached the goal of my walk —a monumental tree that resembled an oak. It had a massive, rough-barked trunk, buttress roots and a span of wide-spreading, tree-sized branches. Running from this tree to another tree 150 feet away was an aerial bridge, hung 50 or 60 feet up. The bridge, a spidery-looking contraption of planks suspended from thin cables, had been constructed so biologists could have a close-up view of life in the forest canopy. I climbed the metal ladder leading to the bridge and moved gingerly out onto the swaying walkway.

Several small cages hung from the cables. One contained a hamster, another a bedraggled chicken. In a third cage a spider monkey lay as if dead. The fourth cage housed a monkey that seemed quite demented; it banged its water dish insistently, spun around its tiny prison like a dervish, stopped for a moment to stare at me, then returned to compulsive motion. A fifth cage was partly covered with netting. Curious about the

Denizens of Panama's rain forest, these five insects are effective predators despite their tiny sizes. The largest, the one-and-a-half-inch Paraponera ant, immobilizes its prey with a sting. So does the half-inch-long Oxyopidae spider, which cannot spin a web; it is shown here overpowering a Heliconius butterfly twice its size. The Asilid fly employs its two powerful front legs to trap other insects. All five insects can inflict irritating bites on humans.

ASILID FLY WITH WOOD NYMPH

OXYOPIDAE PEUCETIA AND VICTIM

TIGER BEETLE

ODONTOMACHUS ANT

PARAPONERA ANT

inmate, I lifted the netting—and came face to face with a two-toed sloth. It turned toward me with excruciating slowness; its eyes, only inches away from mine, seemed filled with malevolence.

The sloth had good reason for hatred, if it could be said to feel that. For its purpose here was to be feasted upon by mosquitoes and to have its blood periodically drawn for examination. Its fellow captives were here for the same reason: to act as sentinels against the lethal enemy known as Yellow Jack.

North Americans call it yellow fever now, and tend to think of it as a disease of bygone times, like the bubonic plague. Yet the virus survives in South America, where it is carried by the mosquito *Haemogogus,* which transmits the disease to monkeys and perhaps to sloths and other creatures of the jungle canopy. Once every decade or two, Yellow Jack moves up out of the South American jungles, across the great Atrato swamp of Colombia, and onto the isthmus of Panama. It was making just such an advance now. The scientists of the Gorgas lab field station were monitoring its progress by means of the animals caged on the aerial bridge, and were laying plans to block the northward march of the virus with insecticides and by clearing the forest. For if yellow fever reached the borders of an urban area, it would be picked up by another mosquito, *Aëdes aegypti,* which breeds in old tires, empty tin cans and other flotsam of civilization; and from *aegypti* it would be transmitted to the close-packed people of the cities. The cities of Panamá and Colón are full of *aegypti.* So, for that matter, are Miami and New Orleans.

Looking at the sloth, and at the demented monkey down the walkway, I was reminded that the jungles of the New World tropics, however much they tantalize man, have always been hostile to his intrusions. The danger has never come from large animals, but it does not take lions or tigers or rampaging elephants to make a country hazardous. The tropical forest has its own multiple means of confounding and repelling invaders. The rain, the heat, the crushing humidity, the dense growth that cannot be penetrated without a machete are only part of the jungle's weaponry. There are, as well, two species of huge pit viper, the bushmaster and the fer-de-lance, and the smaller but no less poisonous green palm viper; there is a tree, *Hura,* whose sap can cause blindness if washed down by rain onto a traveler's face; there are inch-long *Paraponera* ants whose stings can lay a man out; ticks, chiggers, blackflies and mosquitoes in uncountable numbers; and by no means least, diseases like yellow fever, malaria, dysentery and encephalitis.

Europeans, on first encountering the New World jungles, had little idea of how to cope with an environment so radically different from the one they had known. Failure to understand that malaria and yellow fever were borne by mosquitoes, rather than by foul humors in the jungle air, cost the French thousands of lives during the period when they were making an early—and futile—attempt to build a canal across the isthmus. In their hospitals the legs of the beds sat in little cups of water, which not only protected the beds from ants as the French intended, but also provided perfect breeding grounds for mosquitoes. Any man sick enough to be hospitalized had a dim chance of coming out alive. Later, when the Americans took over work on the canal, men continued to die in droves. The chief sanitation officer at the canal, Colonel William Gorgas, finally brought yellow fever and malaria under control, but only after a protracted fight with Washington superiors who scoffed at the idea of mosquitoes as disease spreaders.

The Gorgas story is famous as a triumph over one of the perils of the jungle. But few people have ever heard of another, earlier American effort to challenge the tropical forests in a very different way. In 1854 the United States Navy sent an expedition to find a feasible route for an interocean canal across Darién, the part of the isthmus that lies closest to South America. Virtually unknown in the 19th Century, Darién is a region of low but rugged mountains, tortuous rivers and extensive swamps. Today it is still little known, and remains a formidable barrier between North and South America. The Pan-American Highway, which runs for some 17,000 miles from Fairbanks, Alaska, to Tierra del Fuego, has yet to be completed across Darién. Panamanians call the area *el Tapón*—the Stopper—and the name suits.

The story of the 1854 expedition, preserved in a long account the next year by an American journalist named J. T. Headley, is remarkable on several scores. It abounds with evidence of human endurance, persistence and heroism. At the same time it provides a classic portrait of the jungle as invincible; pitted against its invaders, the Darién rain forest produced just about every weapon in its armory, and prevailed. That there were any survivors at all is astonishing.

The expedition disembarked from the United States Navy corvette *Cyane* on the morning of January 20, 1854, and set out from the shores of Caledonia Bay on the Caribbean coast of Darién. Leading the column of 27 marchers was Lieutenant Isaac Strain, clad in blue Navy flannels and a Panama hat, with a spyglass slung over his shoulder. Strain was a small man, hard-muscled and compact, and at 33 a veteran of previous exploratory expeditions into Brazil and Baja California.

The party was only lightly provisioned, for Strain expected to cross from ocean to ocean in short order. He had made his plans on the basis of reports of an Irish explorer who claimed to have made the journey in just a few hours, by way of a pass only 150 feet high through the mountains of the Great Divide. Strain's men soon found that they had to cut their way inland with machetes, and as for the 150-foot pass through the mountains—the Serranía del Darién—it did not exist. The lowest point the party encountered in the Serranía turned out to be a precipitous 1,500-foot ridge.

The Cuna Indians who inhabited the rain forest were anything but friendly. A proud people who still dwell in Darién and on the San Blas Islands off the Caribbean coast, the Cuna of today continue to resist outside influences on their culture. In Strain's time they were aloof indeed, melting into the jungle ahead of the expedition. The party came upon one village to find the huts in flames, the Indians having set torches to them moments before. In another village the inhabitants had destroyed their canoes with axes to prevent them from falling into the intruders' hands. When Strain finally spotted some Indians, he managed to get their sullen agreement to guide him onward toward the Pacific. But after two days they disappeared.

By the eighth day the expedition was, for all practical purposes, lost in the wilderness. The provisions had dwindled to crumbs of bread and a few pounds of coffee. In the abandoned Cuna villages Strain's hungry crew frequently found abundant stands of plantain—a near relative of the banana—which grows both wild and under cultivation throughout Central America. But Strain, not wishing to give the Indians cause for hostility, refused to let the men eat them. There are other edible fruits and plants in the Darién jungles, including many varieties of fig and a fruit called spondias that is downright ambrosial to the taste. An Indian, or perhaps a present-day botanist, could have survived on them. But Strain was neither Indian nor botanist. The plants were unfamiliar and few were fruiting; this was the dry season. Animals that might be shot for food were difficult to see in the dense forest. Soon the men were near to starving.

Trouble of another sort loomed when the party reached the Río Chucunaque. Though Strain did not know it, the river at that point is no more than 20 miles from the Pacific. But it flows toward the ocean by a serpentine route, so full of twists and turns that the traveling dis-

Culebra Cut, blasted out of a rock saddle 312 fee

high, marks a major breakthrough in the Panama Canal builders' struggle against the mountainous, jungle-covered terrain of the Great Divide.

tance along its banks to the sea is some 100 miles. In places the Chucunaque is so tortuous, running westward for a while, then perversely running eastward, that anyone trying to follow it can lose all sense of direction. And for the Strain party, attempts to find a reliable guide continued to be futile. Few Indians lived on the Chucunaque. Indeed, few live there now; the blackflies are so fierce that for years the only village along the river was called El Martirio—in English, Martyrdom. The Panamanian government more recently has succeeded in relocating some Indians, disposessed by the Bayano Project, to the Chucunaque basin; one of the first buildings constructed was a health clinic.

Strain and his men proceeded to struggle along the banks of the Chucunaque. The river was slow and sluggish in some places, deep and rapid in others. At points sheer rock rose up from the river's edge, but for the most part the banks were thick with undergrowth; one ubiquitous tree, the *piñuela,* or small pineapple, had leaves serrated with spines that produced painful wounds when the men brushed by. Farther in from the shore, the forest was more open, but the vines that hung from every tree and coiled around every bush made walking a torment. The men's feet were lacerated and sore; Strain's were so swollen that it took two men to pull off his boots. At night the flies and mosquitoes drove the explorers half mad. Some of the men tried to lift the expedition's sagging spirits; a seaman named Holmes made a fife out of a reed to play tunes around the campfire, and seaman Lombard piped his bosun's whistle. But the real mood of the party was reflected in the kinds of names they gave to their stopping places along the river: the Camp of the Elephant Mosquitoes, Sorrowful Camp, Noche Triste.

The morning of February 3, two weeks after the expedition had set out, marked a new low point. The provisions were gone. The men had already boiled their last coffee beans four times; now they ate the beans and a monkey they had managed to shoot. Henceforth their fare would consist of whatever their carbines could bring down: an owl, a woodpecker, a crane, hawks. Once they even devoured a long-dead iguana half eaten by maggots. The men killed a vulture, but did not eat it because they could not stand its stench—a fastidiousness they would later overcome. The mainstay of their diet was a nut, surrounded by an acid-tasting pulp, that they discovered on a palm tree. The nuts indeed provided some sustenance, but they also caused stomach cramps and corroded the enamel off teeth.

Marching order began to break down, the men stringing out through the jungle. Their clothes were in tatters; Strain, having given his trousers to another, now traveled in his drawers, with his bare legs providing a banquet for mosquitoes. When several in the party became scarcely able to walk, Strain had a raft built; it was lost in a log jam. A second raft was destroyed in rapids. The men started to build a third, without taking into account a quality of many tropical trees: their wood is heavier than water. The first log they put into the river sank.

Strain concluded that the only hope was for him to press on to the Pacific with some picked men, then bring back boats to rescue the others. He chose three volunteers, left the rest under his second-in-command, Truxton, with orders for them to follow in easy stages, and marched trouserless into the jungle.

Incredibly, Strain accomplished his mission—after almost six agonizing weeks. As he and his three companions struggled on toward the Pacific, keeping as close as they could to the course of the Chucunaque, the jungle visited one of its worst plagues on them—"worms of the woods," probably the larvae of botflies, burrowed into their flesh. These inch-long maggots crawled about beneath the skin, causing excruciating pain. One of the men became so disheartened that only Strain's threat of a flogging kept him going. Yet Strain continued to drive onward, trying to cheer the men by reciting humorous anecdotes from Don Quixote. He built yet another raft, snagged it in some shoals, and built one more that managed to stay afloat.

On the fourth of March, Strain finally reached tidewater. Five days later he and his men, more dead than alive, arrived at the village of Yavisa, near where the river begins to widen into Darién harbor on the Pacific. There the commander of the United States Darién Exploring Expedition, clad only in a blue flannel shirt, one boot and a Panama hat, presented himself to the mayor. That night the mayor gave the newcomers a banquet, which Strain attended in a borrowed petticoat.

At the start of the expedition he had weighed 145 pounds; he now weighed 75. But the man was indomitable. He went on to Darién harbor to seek assistance from a British steam sloop that was anchored there. From the British he obtained a boat armed with a howitzer and manned by 14 British oarsmen. He also recruited some local villagers and a small flotilla of canoes, and embarked on his rescue mission. At the head of tidewater he left the British boat and continued back up the Chucunaque with the canoes, paddling one of them himself.

On March 23 the recruits mutinied, refusing to go farther into a country they knew was hostile. The enraged Strain drew his revolver,

Mistrusting the Indian guides (who subsequently deserted), a member of the ill-fated Strain expedition hacks a notch in a coconut palm to mark the party's position on its harrowing trek across Panama. This illustration, based on survivors' stories, appeared in Harper's New Monthly Magazine *in 1855, a year after the perilous journey through the jungle was completed.*

pointed it at them, and swore that unless they went on he would shoot some of them on the spot. They gave in, paddling farther upriver, and toward sunset that day Strain saw the survivors of his command on the riverbank up ahead.

Of the men he had left behind, five were dead—one of an infection caused by a thorn that had punctured his foot, the rest simply because their strength and spirit had failed. Those who survived were barely alive. Truxton, whom Strain had placed in charge, had decided that the party should turn back toward the Caribbean, but they had been unable to go very far. Increasingly weak, their morale gone, the men had abandoned carbines and haversacks and blankets. Some wandered about temporarily deranged. Some plotted to cannibalize their comrades. Hunger obsessed one and all; one day Truxton, seeing a toad on the ground, seized it, bit off and spit away the head, then devoured the body. At that point Maury, *Cyane's* first assistant engineer, commented, "Well, Truxton, you are getting quite particular; something of an epicure, eh?" He then snatched up the toad's head and devoured it himself.

By the 23rd of March, Truxton knew that five of his men were so weak that they would have to be abandoned on the following morning. But on the evening of the 23rd he heard a shout from Maury, down by the river: *"I see Strain! I see Strain!"*

The next morning, Strain loaded his command of living cadavers into the canoes and started down the Chucunaque toward the Pacific. On March 26, with the expedition two months and six days out of Caledonia Bay, the canoes rounded the bend beyond which lay the waiting British boat. The ordeal was over, though two more of the men would die before reaching the United States. Strain himself, his iron constitution broken by the jungle, would fall sick with fever on a subsequent trip to Panama and die at the age of 36.

Standing on the swaying aerial bridge at Bayano, I surveyed the labyrinth of forest below me and marveled that Strain and his men had managed to get through at all. I wondered how much less their suffering and their losses would have been if they had been adequately prepared and provisioned. But even in the 20th Century, with its dazzling technology, the jungle fights back. In 1972 a well-equipped British expedition set out to cross the 250-mile stretch of tropical wilderness that then separated the points where the northern section of the Pan-American Highway ended and the southern section began. Travel on foot was not part of the plan; the members of the expedition proposed to cross in a pair of four-wheel-drive Range-Rovers. They advanced primarily by winching the vehicles from tree to tree. The Rovers finally did get through—with the aid of 28 horses and motorized rubber boats and liberal assistance from helicopters. At that, the 250-mile journey took 99 days.

It was near dusk now in the jungle at Bayano. In the forest canopy around the aerial bridge the mosquitoes were moving. One hovered near my arm. It was small and dark, almost black: *Haemogogus*, the initial carrier of yellow fever. I brushed it away, but in a moment there was another. Below the bridge, the smaller of the two sentinel monkeys was going crazy again, caroming around inside its little cage. Just before climbing down, I had an urge to go down the walkway, open the cage, and turn the animal back to the jungle.

But of course I didn't.

4/ Searching for Rima

The mysterious melody began. Was it, I asked myself, inviting me to follow? And if I obeyed, to what delightful discoveries or frightful dangers might it lead? WILLIAM HENRY HUDSON/ *GREEN MANSIONS*

In *Green Mansions,* William Henry Hudson's great romantic novel of the American tropics, the young hero, Abel, is lured into the jungle by the haunting call of an unseen bird. He is so stirred by the beauty of the song that he follows its mysterious source deeper and deeper into the forest, and eventually he discovers that the singer is not a bird at all, but a lovely half-wild girl named Rima, who has learned to mimic the sounds of the birds around her.

Like Abel, I too have walked the jungle in quest of unseen singers of beautiful songs. For the bird life of the New World tropics is so rich, so varied—and often so elusive—that it sometimes seems as if Rima herself is calling from every tree. Now she sings in a voice that is bubbling and gay, now she calls mournfully, now she croons, now she scolds, now she utters a scream. But always her voice beckons, always it draws me a little farther into the darkness of the forest, while the singer remains invisible, up ahead in the trees somewhere, a tantalizing, disembodied voice.

The urge to search for Rima attracts hundreds of pilgrims to Central America every year. In Costa Rica alone, a country half the size of Ohio, there are over 760 species of birds, as many as exist in the United States and Canada combined. For Central America, the total is about 1,000 species, the majority in the tropical forests and the rest in open woodland and grassland, on swampy coasts and in fresh-water marshes.

The birds come in an extraordinary range of forms and in colors so brilliant as to make their brightest cousins of the temperate zone seem drab by comparison. Even their names have an exotic ring: scarlet-thighed dacnis, crested guan, uniform crake, jabiru, violaceous trogon, tody motmot, lanceolated monklet, lineated foliage-gleaner, bright-rumped attila, black-capped pygmy tyrant, common potoo.

No bird watcher is immune to the fascination of such names. Certainly I am not, for I have been an unreconstructed bird watcher all my life. To understand my particular affliction, and my excitement upon arriving in Central America, it is necessary to understand just what a bird watcher is, and is not. Bird lovers are people who put up feeders outside their windows and see to it that the chickadees have plenty of sunflower seeds to get through the winter. Ornithologists are people who actually watch birds—that is, study their behavior, their physiology, their environment. Many bird watchers—or birders, as we generally call ourselves—do not, as a rule, really watch birds. Instead, we try to identify in the field as many different species as possible; we collect the sightings of birds, as some people collect stamps.

Bird watchers may not know very much about the habits of birds, but we do know a great deal about how to tell one kind from another. That is what the game is all about. Since it is a sport without trophies or tangible symbols of competence beyond the list of species seen, bird watchers tend to be fanatical compilers of lists. A serious birder will keep a life list (a roster of every species he has seen and when and where he saw it), a United States list, a state list, an annual list, and lists for such special occasions as peak migration days and the traditional Christmas Bird Count—the tally made throughout North and Central America around the holiday time.

The most seasoned practitioners of the sport—the Babe Ruths of bird watching—have life lists of 4,000 or more names. (There are 8,600 bird species in the entire world.) I am no more than a respectable sand-lot player myself. At the time I arrived in Central America my life list for the United States, collected over 30 years, stood at 401 species; my foreign lists—in a shameful state of disarray—came to perhaps 150 more. In Central America I hoped to add at least 200 new species, 300 if I were lucky.

I made my first sortie into the field in Palo Verde, a tract of tall, dry forest and scattered patches of fresh-water marsh, on the Pacific side of Costa Rica above the Península de Nicoya. Palo Verde is a field station of the Organization for Tropical Studies, a consortium involving

22 North American and four Central American universities and supported by the National Science Foundation and a number of private organi-
zations. At the station I met Jim Karr, an ecologist who offered to let me
tag along as a birder while he pursued his field studies the next morning.

During the evening at the station I swatted mosquitoes and studied
my illustrated field guides and printed check lists of birds endemic to
the region. On my list for Costa Rica I found, among other items, 50 different species of hummingbirds, 45 species of tanagers and 72 species
of flycatchers. The sheer size of the bird population has spurred a competition to survive; but thanks to the wide variety of habitats the
various species have been able to specialize and thrive. There is a flycatcher that eats berries, a woodpecker that eats fruit and an epicurean
kite with a bill like an *escargot* fork that dines on nothing but snails.
There are hummingbirds with short bills, long bills, straight bills and
curved bills, each a specialist in harvesting food from flowers of a particular size and shape; there is even a sharp-beaked species called the
purple-crowned fairy that cuts holes in the bases of blossoms and si-
phons off the nectar.

Lying under my mosquito net on the station's long porch that night, I
had trouble getting to sleep. From the forest and the marsh came the
night sounds of birds. I heard a warble, then a sweet, gentle cry, finally
a mad, high-pitched laugh from the darkness. As I listened to the calls,
my mind spun slowly with the names of the birds I might see in the
morning, and grew populous with characters born of my own whimsy:
*Tody Motmot, ex-pro wrestler turned hit man for the mob . . . Brigadier
Uniform Crake, commander on the northern frontier, who with his loy-
al Gurkha Sergeant Major Jabiru fought a sanguinary campaign against
the warlike Guans and Trogons . . . Scarlet-thighed Dacnis, the famous Gold Coast courtesan . . . I dare to love you, madam, though I am
but a common potoo. . . .*

We left the station in the cool of dawn. Far out, against the dark ridges
of the Península de Nicoya, egrets flew in long white skeins. As we
drove along a muddy track in a tough little all-terrain vehicle called an
Automule, I could see chartreuse wings fluttering above the nearby
marsh, and I asked Jim to stop. "Jacanas," he said. I picked up one of
the birds in my glasses; it floated above the water like a butterfly, then
alighted on some lily pads to stroll about on long-toed feet. It was
a new bird for me.

And then in a moment there was another—a head with a long curved

*The small birds that brighten the
Central American jungles thrive on an
abundance of fruit, insects and small
amphibians. Their food-gathering
methods vary widely. The jacamar, for
example, snaps up insects in mid-
air with an audible click of its beak.
The chlorophonia plucks berries and
squeezes them in its bill, letting
the juices trickle down its throat. The
attila, like its namesake a ruthless
killer, devours its frog victims after
dashing them against trees or rocks.*

BLUE HONEY CREEPER

RUFOUS-TAILED JACAMAR

GOLDEN-BROWED CHLOROPHONIA

SOUTHERN LONG-TAILED MANAKIN

SHORT-BILLED TOUCAN

BROAD-BILLED MOTMOT

BRIGHT-RUMPED ATTILA

AZURE-HOODED JAY

beak sticking up above the marsh grasses. "Limpkin," said Jim. I wanted to stay and watch for a while, but Jim was anxious to get past the marsh into the forest beyond, and so he drove on, while I jotted the names of my new birds in my notebook.

Down in a dark, jungly little draw, we came to the place where Jim had set his mist nets—gossamer snares that could entrap a bird without injuring it. Jim wanted to learn something about the diversity of species on or near the forest floor, and since the birds were difficult to see in the dense growth of brush, the nets served to catch them as they moved about; Jim would then mark and release them. The nets, arranged in a circle that loosely enclosed about an acre, had been left rolled up overnight so that no birds would be caught when Jim wasn't there to set them free. Now, with a deft whipping motion of his wrist, he unfurled the nets and began to string them taut between poles. Each net made a wall about 12 yards long and eight feet high. No more visible than a spider's web, the mesh was made of a thread so fine it could be seen only if the sun happened to glint across it.

As we reached the last of the nets, Jim stopped and pointed into the darkness of the forest. I looked and looked, and finally saw something clinging to the side of a tree—a rust-colored bird about the size of my hand, with a long curved bill. "Ruddy woodcreeper," Jim said. "Now that should be a sign there are army ants around."

Like many tropical birds, he explained, the woodcreeper is a specialist. It is, in effect, a professional camp follower, sustaining itself by hovering around columns of army ants and snapping up insects that emerge from the ground cover as they try to flee the advancing ants.

As it turned out, spotting the woodcreeper was the first in a chain of events that flowed, one into another, with grim logic. We followed the woodcreeper for a while until, just as Jim had forecast, we suddenly found ourselves in the midst of a vast formation of army ants, the military precision for which they are named evident in the probing columns and patrols that surrounded us. The ants were not particularly large, but they were incredibly numerous. Shiny brown two-inch-wide trains snaked across the dead leaves on the forest floor; others overran the brush and ascended the tree trunks.

Some ants moved against the tide of the columns, bearing back the booty of the campaign in their jaws: small isopods, and the dismembered legs and bodies of larger insects. Here and there in the columns were soldier ants, larger than the others, with outsize heads to contain

A column of army ants advances along a path it has cleared through gravel on the jungle floor. Such columns are guarded in their line of march by half-inch-long soldiers whose wicked mandibles (top) can fatally wound other insects. Army ants—workers as well as soldiers—not only bite and sting but frequently use the maneuver of mass attack to overwhelm such outsize foes as scorpions and frogs.

the powerful muscles that control their mandibles. These soldiers are so tenacious in their attack and their jaws so powerful that Indians once used them to suture wounds. The ant would be held over the wound and its body squeezed so that its muscles contracted and its jaws clamped the flesh together; the body would then be pinched off.

Stepping very carefully, Jim and I followed the trail of the columns until we found the swarm, or main war party. Here the ants formed a rough circle about 10 yards in diameter with columns radiating from the perimeter. The whole mass marched through the trees on a broad front. From a short distance it looked as if the leaf-littered forest floor itself were slowly shifting and moving. All around I heard faint popping sounds. I realized that the noise was made by grasshoppers and other insects that were jumping up through the dry leaves, trying to escape from the advancing ants. There was something about those faint sounds that was as disturbing as a scream.

Suddenly a creature scurried along in front of the swarm—a rather large scorpion. Formidable in its own right, with a powerful sting, it was no match for the ants. In a moment it stopped and began to writhe as if in agony, stinger arched up over its back. An ant was burrowed against the scorpion's abdomen.

Had the scorpion ignored its attacker and scurried on it might have survived. As it happened, however, the scorpion paused, only for a second or two, but that was too long—a half dozen more ants were at it, then a dozen. In a moment the scorpion had become a pulsing ball of ants, only its stinger emerging to thrash about. Beneath the mass of ants I could sense the creature squirming, fighting for its life, but soon the struggle ceased, and the inexorable march of the ants continued.

I was stunned by the speed and ease with which the ants had killed the scorpion. It had been no contest at all. I felt a little uneasy standing right in the midst of the columns, but Jim assured me that the ants were no danger to humans or other large animals—we could simply move out of range in a few steps. He warned me, however, that the ants can attack from either end—they bite *and* sting—and either form of attack on the human hide can be painful. The ants raid human habitations at the edge of the jungle periodically, he said, and when this happens the people clear out. Such raids are not regarded as unmitigated evils, for the ants clean out cockroaches and other vermin as thoroughly as any exterminator might.

The ants had distracted us for some time. The mist nets needed to be tended now—Jim did not like to leave birds stuck in the mesh for any longer than necessary—and we began to make the rounds. In one of the nets, struggling feebly, was a ruddy woodcreeper—perhaps the same bird that had led us to the ants in the first place. Carefully Jim disengaged the bird from the fine mesh. "Don't worry, kid," he said, "we won't hurt you." He put the woodcreeper in a plastic bag and weighed it on a delicate pocket scale he carried for a separate study he is making of the amount of energy Costa Rican birds expend; then, before releasing the bird, he clipped the tips of a wing feather and a tail feather with a pair of scissors. In this way, Jim explained, he could keep a check on birds that were netted a second time.

As we continued on around the net line, there was a screech from a tree nearby and I looked up to see a good-sized hawk. I put my glasses on the bird. A sleek, handsome creature, it had a gray back, a rufous-barred abdomen, a big murderous beak and a bright yellow eye that glared at us warily. The hawk screamed again and again, its harsh cry much like that of the red-shouldered hawk so common in the lowland forests of the United States. Jim identified the bird as a roadside hawk, a common enough species throughout Central America, but still a new one for my life list.

I thought nothing more about the hawk at the time, but about an hour later, as we approached another net, we could see that something had gone wrong. Two big balls of leaves were stuck in the mesh, and so were two dead woodcreepers; apparently the leaves had been kicked up into the net during some kind of struggle.

Jim began to disengage one of the birds. "I think that hawk got in here and killed them," he said. "Damn, it makes me mad, I hate to kill a bird. See this one?" He held up the little bundle of limp feathers and spread the wings. "The clipped feathers—it's the one we caught a while ago. Damn! The problem is, this can become a habit. That hawk might hang around now."

We continued our circuit of the nets, occasionally dodging the columns of army ants that by now seemed to be probing everywhere in our piece of jungle. Underneath a fallen log we discovered the ants' bivouac—a seething ball of ants about 18 inches in diameter. Army ants live in a cycle: for a period of about two weeks they are nomadic, bivouacking in a new site each night and hunting over a new stretch of ground each day. Then they enter a stationary phase for nearly three weeks. Although raiding parties still go out daily, many of the ants remain at the bivouac to protect the queen while she lays thousands of eggs. Jim poked at the ball with a short stick. Ants and white cocoons came spilling out, and suddenly Jim began slapping at his hand. "Got me," he grimaced, and held up his hand. The flesh at the web of his thumb was swelling with an angry welt.

We backed off from the bivouac and continued along the line of nets. In one of them another woodcreeper was enmeshed. It began calling plaintively as Jim freed it, and within seconds I heard a rush of heavy wings. The roadside hawk lit in a nearby tree and glared at us, and at the woodcreeper.

"There's our killer," I said. "You devil," Jim said harshly. He released the woodcreeper with an underhand toss into low brush where the hawk would have trouble following. The hawk kept its perch, but it seemed to understand perfectly well what was going on—the nets were a free-lunch counter.

Only 15 minutes later, we heard a scream from the forest, and when we raced back we found a panicked woodcreeper caught in the mesh and the hawk perched nearby. "What we've got now is a professional killer in the nets," Jim said. He shook his head. "There's nothing to do but close up shop."

Soberly Jim started taking down and folding his nets. I followed, helping where I could and mulling over the events of the morning. The woodcreeper made its living from the army ants and thus had led us to see them and to witness the death of the scorpion. We in turn had led the woodcreeper to its own death in the talons of the hawk. And the hawk, quicker than we were at finding birds in the nets, had now driven us from the field. We had gone there simply as spectators on the natural scene. But this morning I had learned that in the dynamic and interlocking life system of the jungle, spectators were apt to become participants in a deadly game.

In subsequent weeks, as I traveled in Costa Rica and elsewhere in Central America, I greedily accumulated new birds for my life list. I spotted a chlorospingus and a chlorophonia, a cotinga and a tityra, a bananaquit, a peppershrike and a great kiskadee. Back home in the United States, I very rarely see any bird I haven't seen before. But now I was seeing new birds every day I spent in the field. My life list increased by 40 species, 60, 80, 100.

There were moments of beauty—really the only justification for this odd hobby—beauty so intense as to seem almost transcendent. Dawn on the ocean off Puntarenas, and overhead a frigate bird on scimitar wings sliding into the first rays of the sun. In the jungle at Palo Verde, a great clattering from the treetops and then a pair of scarlet macaws arrowing past, their plumage so brilliant against the green of the jungle that it shocked the eye. High over grassy fields near the Pacific shore, a white-tailed kite, breast and tail glinting like snow in the sunshine as it hung suspended from quickly beating wings, then dropped in a long, slow vertical dive toward the earth.

But there were frustrations, too. For every bird that I saw, a dozen eluded me. Strange cries came constantly from the jungle, Rima calling from the darkness of the forest.

Again and again, in the mountains of Costa Rica, I heard a sound like a hammer clanging on an anvil. I knew that this was the call of the bellbird, a species that migrates vertically from the lowlands to breed in the cloud forests of the volcanic highlands; as long as the sun is up, the sentinel male bird repeats its loud, clear call. But though I peered up into the canopy of intertwined leaves till my neck got stiff, I was never able to spot the performer. Toward dusk in the lowland jungles, I often heard lunatic laughter that went on compulsively, as if the owner of the voice had been gripped with hysteria. A laughing falcon, perhaps? Who knows?

My search finally led me to another field station of the Organization for Tropical Studies, a place called La Selva—"The Jungle"—in the Caribbean lowlands of Costa Rica. I had heard that one birder had seen over 100 species in a single day at La Selva—an astonishing number, considering the difficulty of spotting birds in the dense, wet forest. And I wanted to see how well I could do myself. I reached the station after a three-hour drive on a bad road through the mountains from San José and a short trip up a muddy river in a dugout canoe. Next morning, the calls of pauraques, sounding like whippoorwills as they ended their nocturnal hunt for insects, woke me long before dawn.

At La Selva, a velvet lives in the clearing where birders go to do their watching. The velvet moves about at night, but in the daylight hours it rests in a loose coil of burnished brown on the forest floor, waiting silently with jaws full of death for whatever may come along.

The Costa Ricans call this lethal creature *terciopelo*, the Spanish for "velvet." Its more common name, originally a French one, is the fer-de-lance. At La Selva one of these big vipers had made its home in a patch of land from which the underbrush and small trees had been cleared to form a kind of arboretum of tall trees. The fer-de-lance had been seen there frequently, usually coiled near a fallen log or some other cover.

A laughing falcon, capable of a call that sounds like mad human hilarity, maintains a moment's silence as it scouts for snakes, its chief prey. When it spots a potential victim on the ground, the bird swiftly descends and uses one outstretched wing as a shield until it can clutch the snake behind the head with one foot and peck it to death with its sharp, potent beak.

When I announced one morning that I planned to go bird watching in the clearing, three different people advised me to walk carefully and keep my eyes peeled. Since my advisers were all tropical biologists, not given to excessive fear of snakes, I took their warning seriously. I am not afraid of snakes either, at least not in any phobic way, but even the most rational man must respect the fer-de-lance; it grows to a length of as much as nine feet and is very aggressive. Its bite can be fatal—its powerful venom dissolves nerve tissue and destroys blood cells and artery walls—and those who survive may suffer paralysis or tissue damage so massive as to require amputation of the bitten limb.

And so at dawn I entered the arboretum, one slow foot after the other, tapping the ground before me with a long stick, like a blind man crossing a street. I did not carry the stick as a weapon against the snake. I had no desire to kill it; I just wanted to make the velvet reveal itself before I stepped on it.

I could hear birds in the big trees, and occasionally I saw the flicker of wings in the canopy far above. I advanced across the clearing, tap, tap, tap, trying to keep one eye on the trees and the other on the ground ahead of me. There was a croak like a frog's, and then I saw that it came from an enormous black bird flying overhead—a Swainson's toucan, one of the most flamboyant of all Central American birds. Because of their huge yellow beaks, the toucans are sometimes called flying bananas, and indeed, the one I saw did appear to be carrying a monstrous banana in its bill.

Ahead of me some large, pendulous objects hung from the branches of a tall tree. Perhaps four feet long and shaped like elongated gourds, they were the intricately woven grass nests of a colony of oropendolas. I looked at the nests through my glasses; there was no activity around them. But in a moment I heard some oropendolas calling—a loud, burbling cry that sounded as if it came from underwater—and in a distant tree I saw a couple of the black, crow-sized birds thrashing about.

I had learned something of the home life of the oropendolas from a scientist named Neal Smith, who had spent four years studying colonies of the birds in Panama and trying to solve the mystery of their relationship with the giant cowbird, a species that parasitizes oropendola nests. The story Smith told me was yet another astonishing illustration of the complexity of relationships between creatures in the tropics.

The giant cowbirds of Central America build no nests of their own, but scatter their eggs in the beautifully constructed hanging nests of the oropendolas, usually after the oropendola has deposited a single egg. The presence of the cowbird egg inhibits the oropendola from laying another of her own—two eggs is her usual clutch. The cowbird egg hatches first, and since the cowbird chick is precocious and aggressive, it deprives the more passive oropendola chick of some of its food. Thus it might be assumed that the oropendola comes out the loser in its relationship with the cowbird.

However, Smith has found that the truth is a great deal more complicated. First, he discovered that among the oropendolas there are two distinct types of behavior. In some colonies, the male oropendola usually drives the female cowbird away before she has an opportunity to deposit an egg; if, however, the cowbird succeeds in laying, the oropendola frequently destroys the egg before it hatches. Smith calls these aggressive oropendolas "discriminators." But in other colonies the oropendolas are "nondiscriminators"—that is, they do not prevent the cowbird from entering the nest and laying an egg. The oropendolas then dutifully raise the young parasite chick along with their own.

This seemed inexplicable—until Smith noticed that in every discriminator colony, the oropendola nests are close to the nests of wasps or bees. But the nondiscriminators—those that accept the cowbird chicks into their homes—do not have wasps or bees as neighbors.

Could there, Smith wondered, be a relationship between the presence of wasps and bees, and the attitude of the oropendolas toward cowbirds? On further investigation, Smith learned that the major cause of mortality among oropendola chicks is the larvae of botflies. The chicks are born without a protective downy coat, and the flies lay their eggs directly on the skin of the newly hatched birds; the larvae eventually burrow into the young bird's flesh and kill it. The botflies, however, appear to be wary of wasps and bees—particularly of the bees, which hover nearby all day in a noisy, buzzing swarm. Thus the oropendolas that have wasps and bees for neighbors are protected from the attacks of botflies. These colonies chase away the cowbirds.

In the nondiscriminator colonies, it proved to be the young cowbirds themselves that control the botflies. Like all birds, the adult oropendolas make no effort to preen their young. It is the lively baby cowbirds that preen their passive oropendola nestmates and snap hungrily at anything tiny that moves in the nest, including botflies and their larvae.

The implications of all this are inescapable, if mind boggling. The oropendolas somehow sense that the cowbirds are a threat to their reproductive success, but that the botflies are an even greater threat. Thus, in the colonies that are not protected against botflies by the pres-

A fer-de-lance uncoils menacingly, its javelin-shaped head weaving. The snake is one of several Central American pit vipers—another is the bushmaster—which have a small depression, or pit, between eye and nostril. Through nerve endings in the pit the vipers sense minute changes of temperature that betray the proximity of warm-blooded prey. After killing with a venomous strike, the fer-de-lance swallows its victim whole.

ence of wasps or bees in the neighborhood, the oropendolas accept the cowbirds as the lesser of two evils. Even though they make a dent in the oropendola chicks' diet, they provide the most effective line of defense against the flies.

As I stood in the clearing at La Selva watching the oropendolas fly in and about the treetops across the way, it seemed to me barely credible that these big, noisy birds could behave in accordance with such complex logic. But they did. Somehow in their collective intelligence they had discovered a syllogism for survival.

I spent an hour in the clearing, but perhaps because I was distracted by the thought of the fer-de-lance lurking there, I saw few other birds. Finally I decided to leave the clearing and try another spot.

I had already learned, elsewhere, that the deep heart of the jungle is not the best place to look for birds. The problem is that you cannot see the trees for the forest. The eye is baffled by the complex, disorganized patterns of shadow and light; visual sensitivity is smothered in a profound ocean of greenness. The bird watcher in the tropics becomes a seeker of clearings, a creeper along edges. And so I headed now for another clearing, where the entire forest had been cut back a few years before during one of La Selva's studies of tropical plant growth.

Earlier that morning I had attached a couple of pieces of bright red tape to the brim of my hat, hoping that hummingbirds might fly up to see if I was a flower and a source of good things to eat, and thus give me a chance to see them at close range. My ruse was proving successful, up to a point. As I walked along the narrow forest trail toward the clearing, hummingbirds shot past me like bullets. Sometimes they paused by my ear on vibrating wings to give me a once-over, but they were so quick, and gone so fast, that I could barely get my eyes focused on them before they disappeared.

Hummingbirds are certainly among the most charming creatures of the New World tropics. They exist in great profusion and variety—one book lists 91 different species for Central America. They are stunningly pretty; some of the males are bedecked with long streamer tails and iridescent mustachios, beards, visors and helmets. And their names are nothing short of poetry: hairy hermit, violet saberwing, green-crowned brilliant, purple-throated mountaingem, constant starthroat, Buffon's plumeleteer, Barrot's fairy and Lucy's emerald. There are so many species, in fact, that the ornithologists' creative wellsprings have on occasion run dry—at least that is the only explanation I can think of for such names as the lovely hummingbird, charming hummingbird, admirable hummingbird and adorable coquette.

These tiny high-speed machines are incredible examples of avian evolution and adaptation. They beat their wings in cycles as fast as 79 times per second, and alone among birds they generate power on both forward and backward wing strokes—a distinction that allows hummingbirds to stand still in the air or even fly in reverse. They have a pulse rate as high as 1,260 beats per minute, a breathing rate as high as 273 respirations per minute.

They function at such an intense pitch and expend so much energy that they consume extraordinary amounts of food to fuel their tiny bodies. In his book on hummingbirds, the eminent ornithologist Alexander Skutch relates a time he ate sparingly at a luncheon in Guatemala, and was accused by his host of having an appetite like a hummingbird. "It's fortunate," Skutch replied with suitable solemnity, "that I do not have an appetite like a hummingbird. If I did, you might not invite me to visit you again. I would eat more than 300 pounds of food daily!"

Indeed, in one experiment a white-eared hummingbird, in a period of 16 hours, consumed 856 per cent its own weight in food and water. In order to keep from exhausting their slim food reserves, hummingbirds become torpid at night; their metabolism slows and their temperature drops until they are in a state similar to hibernation. In this condition they are incapable of flight, and if disturbed may need as long as an hour to recover and fly away.

This morning, though, the hummingbirds seemed to like using the trail as a flight path, and they kept buzzing in, giving my hat inquisitive examinations, and darting away before I could identify their particular species. I moved on along the trail, trying to keep my eyes peeled for movements in the undergrowth. I heard a buzzing sound, spied a motion back in the deep shadows and found a tiny bird in my glasses. I called its field marks out loud so I would remember them: "Rufous back, very short tail, black cap, black-and-white striped cheeks, gray breast." Then I dropped my binoculars and started frantically thumbing through my field guide. The bird turned out to be a gray-breasted wood wren, a new species for me. A few minutes later I spotted another little bird and thumbed the book once more. Orange-billed sparrow, another new one. By the time I reached the clearing I had picked up a third, a buff-rumped warbler. After a slow start it was turning out to be a good morning.

The clearing looked like another probable fer-de-lance habitat, and so I started poking ahead of me with the stick again. Across the clearing, I saw a small bird flutter delicately out from the branch of a tall tree, spin about in the air and then return to its high perch. I locked the glasses on it just as it flew out in another sortie; it was a tiny black-and-white flycatcher, with a pair of long, slender tail feathers that floated behind it in the air. When I checked my list I found that it was called a long-tailed tyrant—a fearsome name for such a dainty creature.

In a clump of low bushes ahead of me, I caught a flurry of movement. A bird was in there, but I couldn't spot it through the close-packed foliage. Tapping my fer-de-lance stick ahead of me, I moved forward slowly. I began to make squeaking sounds by sucking air through my pursed lips—a standard bird-watcher's ploy to attract inquisitive songbirds and lure them into coming up close. Suddenly I was conscious of the picture that I made. I was a grown man, generally considered sane by my friends and colleagues. But here I was, tapping along like a blind man, squeaking like a mouse, and wearing a hat festooned with red tapes in hope of convincing some small bird that I was in fact a flower. I could not blame anyone who concluded that my brains had been scrambled by the sun.

In the bush ahead the bird popped into view. "Olive yellow," I called out loud. "Larger than a sparrow, thick bill, black mask on face and throat." I dropped my binoculars and fumbled for my field guide. By the time I discovered that the bird I had seen was a black-faced grosbeak and another new species for my list, my self-consciousness had retreated back to where it belonged.

Some Singular Simians

Of all the animals that tenant the Central American jungles, by far the most captivating are the monkeys. They are also the liveliest, shattering the silence with their calls, flitting from tree to tree on daily food hunts, playfully roughhousing, sometimes pausing to peer through the branches at intruders (right). Six distinct species, from one to 16 pounds in size, make up the monkey population, and their habitats range from the top of the forest canopy to the scrubby undergrowth on the jungle floor.

All six species, along with 60 others in South America, belong to a group known as New World monkeys, which distinguishes them from the so-called Old World monkeys across the Atlantic and Pacific. Both evolved from a single simian group that appeared about 40 million years ago in Africa and Asia. Some of its members migrated to North America; later pioneers pushed on to Central and South America. Those that remained in the north eventually died out as the climate became colder, but the emigrants in the south flourished, gradually evolving into their present forms.

Despite their common ancestry, New and Old World monkeys differ markedly in their physical characteristics. The Old World monkey's nose is narrow, the New World's broad, with widely spaced nostrils. A prehensile tail—in effect a fifth hand, convenient for grasping and holding on to branches—is lacking in Old World species. Of the six Central American species, the cebus, howler and spider monkey enjoy this appendage. Another baffling distinction is that while some New World monkeys give birth to twins and triplets, the phenomenon is rare among their Asian and African relatives. And no Old World male ever takes the mothering role, a not-uncommon practice in the New World.

All of Central America's monkeys are, in fact, endowed with a highly developed social sense. Each species pursues its own, well-ordered way of group living, some in simple family units and others in bands of up to 30. Because they occupy different niches in the forest, the species seldom meet. Only when paths cross in the search for the fruits, leaves and insects on which the monkeys feed do they defend their territories. Even then the defense adds up to more sound than fury—the cacophony of howls, squeaks, whistles and chatterings that are the jungle's most celebrated aural hallmark.

A loose-limbed spider monkey— most widespread of Central America's simian species—eyes an unexpected visitor. At such encounters spider monkeys may either flee or cautiously approach, often rattling branches or screeching to prove their fearlessness.

A marmoset pair engages in the pleasurable and hygienic activity of mutual grooming, a standard practice of males and females of the species. Among other monkeys, the male may be groomed by his mate without ever having to reciprocate.

A squirrel monkey maneuvers a tricky walkway as nimbly as its rodent namesake. Unlike most simians that forage during the daytime, the squirrel monkey is constantly on the go, rarely resting at midday and sometimes eating on the run.

A Trio of Peewees near the Forest Floor

The three smallest primates of the Central American rain forest—night monkeys, marmosets and squirrel monkeys—stake out the jungle understory and its low-growing trees and shrubs. There, reasonably safe from such foes as hawks and falcons, they scurry about on all fours, using their tails for balance on narrow arboreal runways.

The squirrel monkeys, the most gregarious, form bands of as many as 30 individuals. The band has no dominant leader, but an echelon of watchful males lives on the periphery of the group, while females and young remain well inside the lines.

The night monkeys, so named because they forage after dark, live in small family units consisting usually of the parents, one or more infants and juveniles up to about three years old. The night monkey tends to be more feisty than other monkeys in protecting its brood; it will not just drive off intruders but may attack them as well—even when they are of its own species.

Marmosets also live in small families, but the male parent assumes a major role in child rearing—carrying, playing with and even feeding infants when they are old enough to take solid food. His responsibilities are disproportionate to his size: smallest of the small monkeys, an adult marmoset weighs a pound at most and measures no more than about 10 inches from the head to the base of the tail.

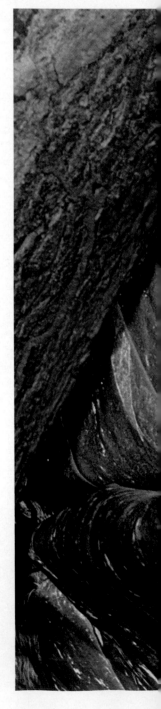

Startled by the photographer's flash, a night monkey stares through the foliage. In the morning, it will retire to sleep in a tree hollow.

Prying Eyes and White Faces

The cebus, sometimes called the capuchin for its monklike cowl and dark pate, is perhaps the smartest and certainly the most inquisitive among Central America's simians. Although the species lives in bands of between 10 and 25 members, individuals are constantly on the prowl, poking around and investigating anything that appears new or different about their jungle habitat.

Resourcefulness is another one of their traits. When a cebus comes upon a cluster of ripe fruits, it will carry off three or four for future eating, rather than make a quick snack of one fruit right then and there; in probing for insects, it will turn over rotting bark or brush aside leaves rather than simply settling for the insects that easily come to hand.

In the early years of this century the cebus was a familiar sight to city dwellers, many of whom nostalgically remember it as the costumed, cup-rattling organ-grinder's monkey.

A male cebus—weight about seven pounds—confidently straddles a palm frond.

A cebus diligently grooms a member of its band. The cleansing process is vital for this species because of its habit of ranging far and wide—and thus picking up great quantities of dirt, leaf scraps, rotted wood and insect pests.

A howler mother, baby on back and youngster at side, enjoys a respite.

A Loud-mouthed Heavyweight

Every morning at dawn a raucous chorus splits the jungle air: high in the forest canopy, the howler monkeys are greeting the new day. Nor does that put an end to the howling; it is repeated at dusk, and often in between, whenever a leader of a howler group wants to warn its score of members of danger, or discourage trespassers from the group's domain of 20 acres or so.

The heftiest of Central America's monkeys—an adult male may weigh 16 pounds—the howlers are able to produce their characteristic call, a cross between a roar and a bark, due to an enlarged voice box in a unique throat chamber of bone that amplifies sound. The female has a smaller version of the same equipment, but contents herself with loud wails, groans or cries—usually to signal distress or summon a straying infant. But whether the sound is made by male or female, the voice of the howler may be audible for miles.

His prehensile tail steadying his stance, an adult male howler warns of an approaching intruder. The white marks on his neck are botfly larvae that were laid in the monkey's skin as eggs, and that will eventually hatch there.

A full-grown spider monkey, pink mouth agape, indulges in a favorite form of exercise.

The Spectacular Swingers

The spider monkey is the supreme acrobat of the forest canopy, capable of spectacular 30-foot leaps between branches. Much of this virtuosity is due to its extraordinary tail, which is longer than its head and body combined, and which serves as a safety catch at the end of a leap. Another highly functional feature of the tail—lacking in the tail of the cebus monkey—is a tip whose underside is ridged like a human fingerprint. Not only does this provide the spider monkey with added purchase in grasping things, but it is also a sensitive extra implement for probing and picking up small objects such as nuts.

The spider monkey's design for living calls for a small group of varying composition: either a lone female and her young, or a few males with a larger number of females and young, or a few males only. Since the males tend to stay aloof from family life, the females take exceptional care of their offspring, and for up to 10 months—a longer period than most other monkey mothers devote to the task. Infants ride cozily on maternal backs and get a great deal of help in the precarious business of negotiating crossings from branch to branch. But as juveniles, spider monkeys become independent and adept, engaging in lively play, wrestling, chasing one another through the trees for hours each day —honing the acrobatic skills they will employ in adulthood.

Slende

but strong front paws and tail support this monkey's weight.   Its tail securely hooked on a branch, a spider monkey ponders its next leap.

Two adult spider monkeys take a breather after a long morning of strenuous exertion.

A mother makes a bridge of her body to ensure the safety of her baby between trees.

Looking like Hamlet mulling a course of action, this adult spider monkey is more likely prospecting for specks of food imbedded under its fingernails.

An infant snuggles in the maternal bosom. Spider-monkey babies are born with black fur, but in six to 10 months it turns coppery, the adults' color.

Balancing deftly, a female spider monkey begins to groom her mate.

Ready to take a siesta, three spider monkeys form a furry tangle. The monkeys enjoy bodily contact so much that they often bed down in heaps.

5/ Along the Sultry Coast

*A faint air then moved from off shore as though
under the impulse of the pouring light. It was heated and
humid and bore a curious odour, at once foreign and
familiar, a smell of damp earth. I thought that I
had inhaled the very spirit of the tropics of which it was born.*

H. M. TOMLINSON/ *THE SEA AND THE JUNGLE*

The Caribbean coast along the arc from Belize down through Panama is a region quite distinct from the interior of Central America. It is cut off from the more densely populated highlands by miles of low-lying jungle, and the relatively few inhabitants are notably diverse in lineage. There are Creoles, of mixed African and European descent; Black Caribs, whose ancestors were African and Caribbean Indian; Mosquito and Cuna Indians; Mestizos, of mixed Spanish and Amerindian blood; and people of purebred Spanish descent. In recent centuries, the region's ties have been not only to Spain but also to England, whose Caribbean empire once extended to the shores of the isthmus.

The coast is very hot and exceedingly wet; one spot on the Nicaraguan shore has recorded an annual rainfall of 340 inches. From Nicaragua north the coastline is frequently whipped by violent tropical storms. The insect population is formidable, since the chiggers and mosquitoes found inland also flourish here, and their hordes have been reinforced by the sand flies and other insects peculiar to a seaside environment. The few towns are squalid. The roads, insofar as any exist, are impassable mud tracks during much of the year.

And yet this damp and difficult place has a certain magnetism to it. From the shore, coral reefs stretch away as far as the eye can see, and mangrove cays lie like dark cruisers on the horizon. Behind the shore sluggish rivers snake through mangrove swamps. A ceaseless wind rustles in the fronds of coconut palms, and crocodiles bellow in the night.

There is a sense of history here. This was part of the Spanish Main of the conquistadors, and also the haunt of rum runners, gun runners, roistering mahogany cutters, and pirates—Henry Morgan and Edward Teach and the dreaded Frenchman L'Ollonois, who once plucked out the living heart of an enemy and ate it. There is mystery, too, a certain spookiness in the hot, moist air. In coastal villages obeah ladies—voodoo priestesses—practice their own brand of magic, brewing foul batches of blue soup with which to hex their enemies. In the swamps the *wowlah,* as the great boa constrictor is known here, glides through mangrove tangles, and the fer-de-lance lurks at the edges of clearings.

If you should ever get bitten by a fer-de-lance, local people say, you must cut off the serpent's head so the village snake doctor can cure you with a broth made from it. A visitor is cautioned that offshore the spectral merman Dagon lures unsuspecting fishermen to their death. In the jungles the *duendes* dwell—little men covered with long gray hair who will cut off your thumbs if they get a chance, because they have none of their own. The moon here, it is said, has such power that it can decay the meat of slaughtered animals, and at the full its rays can crack the trunks of the mahogany trees in the forest.

Near the northern end of the long coastline, at the base of the Yucatán peninsula, lies the tiny country formerly known as British Honduras, now called Belize. The origin of the latter name is obscure. Some believe that it is a corruption of *be likin,* the Maya words for "the land toward the sea"; and insofar as that phrase seems to suggest a place remote, a place way off there somewhere, it is highly appropriate. "If the world had any ends," Aldous Huxley wrote in the 1930s, "British Honduras would certainly be one of them."

Although things have changed since Huxley's time, they have not changed all that much. Jaguars prowl the jungles and low mountains of the hinterlands, and manatees slide through the dark lagoons. Jabiru storks with seven-foot wing spans circle above the mangroves, flying so high that they are no more than white motes in the sun. Lying offshore, at distances that vary from 20 to 60 miles, is a coral reef that runs the entire length of the country's 170-mile coastline. Next to Australia's, this barrier reef is the longest in the world, an almost-unbroken wall between land and sea. On the land side of the reef the shallow water is turquoise or emerald, mottled with the patterns of coral heads that almost reach the surface. On the other side, the water turns immediately to deep blue as the sea floor plunges abruptly downward.

All along the Belizean coast, between the reef and the littoral, are hundreds of the small islands known as cays, created by the building action of waves, or the accumulation of coral, or the entrapment of soil by the roots of mangroves growing in shallow water. While some of the cays are picture-book islands with tall palm trees and white sand beaches, others are simply coral bars exposed at high tide, or clumps of mangroves with tortuous, interlocking roots.

Some of the cays have wonderful names: Drowned Cay, Hen and Chickens Cay, Last Chance Cay, Spanish Lookout Cay, Man of War Cay, Bread and Butter Cay, Weewee Cay. Others have no name at all. In the cool of one morning, before the sun got truly fierce, a Creole fisherman named Willie Faux and I left the little coastal village of Placentia and headed out toward a nameless cay inside the barrier reef. In fact, this cay did not even exist, Willie told me, until 1961, when the killer hurricane Hattie casually threw it up out of the sea by washing quantities of pipestem coral into deep windrows along an old shoal line.

Willie's boat was one of those motorized dugout canoes that are the main means of getting about the backwaters of Central America. Throughout the Spanish-speaking hinterlands they are called *cayucos* or *canoas,* but in Belize, where English is the predominant tongue, they are known as dories. Willie's dory was a small craft for big water, but the sea was calm and the weather clear. Looking back, I could see the flat green of the coastal rain forest; behind it rose the jagged silhouette of the Cockscomb Range and still farther back was the haze blue of the Maya Mountains. Ahead of us, to the east, the farther cays were separated from the water by mirage, so that they seemed to float above the sea. The cay where we planned to camp lay beyond, over the horizon.

Our cay, when we reached it, turned out to be a desolate place, a slag heap of bleached coral baking in the sun. But it was the best campsite around, Willie said. The other cays, lush and green as they looked, were nothing but mangroves, with no dry land at all, or they abounded in mosquitoes, sand flies, warble flies and doctor flies, which, Willie said, "can give you a real injection."

We pitched camp, then went looking for fish. The water around the cay was shallow and very clear. Looking down, I could see reddish pipestem coral, here and there the big, whorled shells of conch and, on the bottom, huge starfish looking like giant disembodied hands. I trolled a feather streamer behind the boat, and before long I had a strike.

The Turneffe Islands form a circle outside the barrier reef off Belize. Unlike the area's cays, this large atoll was created by faulting.

The fish did not feel like a big one, but it made those determined, head-shaking runs characteristic of the fish called jacks. Common in the coastal waters off Central America, jacks are deep-bodied, voracious predators, and because they are extremely strong and have great endurance, they can be a challenge for any fisherman using light tackle. When I worked the fish up close to the boat I could feel it begin to struggle with a kind of panicky violence, and when I looked down into the water I saw something that shocked me—the long, toothy snout of a barracuda, the biggest I had ever seen. I couldn't have caught *that,* I thought. Just then the line stopped throbbing, and I reeled in a jack of about five pounds. Or rather, I reeled in the front half of a jack that had probably weighed five pounds when it had been an entire fish. Now it was nothing but a head and a string of bloody entrails. The barracuda had savaged it just as I had worked it up to the boat; the frantic, last-minute struggle telegraphed to me by the line had been the jack's adrenalin-charged attempt to escape the barra's rush.

I had lost fish to barracuda on several earlier occasions, for these predators abound in the warm, shallow waters off the Central American coast. Lean and racy, they seem to have little fear of boats or men, and the splashing struggle of a hooked fish triggers them into attack. In these waters barracuda sometimes reach a length of almost six feet and a weight of 60 pounds, but even a 15-pounder is terrifyingly dentured. Superficially a barracuda bears an uncanny resemblance to the freshwater pike, also long and lean with great predacious jaws. Both are lurkers that lie quietly in cover, shooting out like arrows at unsuspecting prey; when they move they are extremely quick in short bursts.

Yet the two fish are totally unrelated. Their similarity is a textbook example of what biologists call convergent evolution—that is, if certain physical forms and food-gathering techniques prove to be effective, they are apt to turn up in different places, in creatures of widely disparate lineage. For example, the penguins of the antarctic and the auks and murres of the subarctic are remarkably similar in form and function, even though they have evolved half a world apart. Similarly, the ancestors of the barracuda in salt water, and of the pike in fresh, both hit on the same formula for survival—that of a lurking, quick-striking predator; as their descendants evolved toward maximum efficiency they came to resemble each other in shape, habits and disposition.

The idea that barracuda are dangerous to human beings may be scoffed in some places, but not on the coast of Belize. Willie Faux told me of two unprovoked attacks he knew about. A European visitor lost part of a foot. A Carib conch fisherman had the arteries of his lower leg severed, and bled to death before reaching a hospital. Both men were attacked while wading in water less than knee deep. It was possible, Willie thought, that in a feeding frenzy the barracuda had chased some bait fish into the shallows, and that a foot splashing through the roiled water looked as edible as anything else.

Willie and I caught no barracuda around the cays on this particular day. But I did catch and release a couple of strong, high-jumping tarpon, which put me into a wonderful mood. Later, back on our little nameless cay, I went to bed under a moon so bright I was quite prepared to believe its beams could crack mahogany.

The wind woke me around five in the morning. Blowing unobstructed across thousands of miles of the Atlantic and the Caribbean, gathering strength as it came, it pounded against the little cay, and the fly of the lightweight tent snapped like a whip cracking. The coral did not hold the tent pegs well, and I began to fear that if one peg pulled out the whole tent might go. I lay uneasily in my sleeping bag, staring at the darkness through the mosquito net and waiting for the dawn.

There was no sunrise, just a gradual lightening of the sky to a somber gray. We got up and made a driftwood fire, crouching beside it to try to get below the main force of the wind. Gusts blew the heat out horizontally, so that a long time passed before the coffee came to a boil. Waiting, we watched whitecaps race past our little island. Shoal water broke the full force of the waves, but we could still feel the coral trembling with their impact. "Looks like it will last all day, mon," Willie said. "Or longer." Even his lilting Creole accent sounded disconsolate.

After breakfast I went for a walk. I had paced off the cay the night before—29 paces wide, 147 paces long. There was no soil, no water, no cover except a half dozen wind-twisted black mangroves and an occasional patch of knotty-looking shrubs that hugged the coral closely. Crusoe would have gone dotty here, I thought. There was no life, no stimuli, nothing to look at or think about.

But then at the far end of the island I saw four pelicans hunkered in the wind. Clumsily, and no doubt reluctantly, they dragged themselves into the air as I approached, and fought their way offshore through the gusts. At the very edge of the water I saw something moving, and when I raised my glasses to focus on it I realized that it was an old friend from the beaches of New York's Long Island—a ruddy turnstone. A plump, plover-like bird in a drab winter coat, it probed into the coral for crustaceans, then scurried backward to escape an incoming wave. The turnstone was even farther from home than I. Not many months before, I had seen members of the species on Long Island, in migration all the way from the shores of Greenland and Northern Canada. And this one in my binoculars had summered there, too, before returning for the winter to this little tropical cay.

As I was watching the turnstone I heard a piercing whistle behind me; turning, I saw the flash of wings as two big birds separated in the air. The bird that had sounded off was an osprey, and it was fleeing from an attacker, a frigate bird. All along the coast of Central America the frigates hang like sinister kites in the wind. With their long slender wings and forked tails they look prehistoric, somehow suggestive of pterodactyls. These aerial pirates eat fish but seldom catch them. Instead, with its mastery of the air the frigate holds a single position in the sky, as if suspended from invisible strings, and from this airborne perch it harries gulls and terns, making them drop their catches.

Even the osprey, strong and armed with formidable talons, normally cannot match the frigate bird on the wing. This morning, though, the osprey flew off powerfully, beating across the wind, with the fish still clutched in its talons. The outcome pleased me. I have always felt a certain brotherhood with the osprey, for we are both fishermen. Frequently the osprey catches fish when I do not, but I bear him no malice; he is, after all, the professional, and I merely the dilettante.

I reached the end of the coral and stood there for a while with the wind stinging my eyes. When I got back to the campfire a little later I was met by a strange procession. Down from the roots of the mangroves onto the sand came marching, in single file, a column of sea shells. Little whelks and conchs of green and blue and russet, they lock stepped down through the roots on tiny feet. I stared at them for a moment before I realized what they were: a battalion of soldier crabs out on a foray, attracted by a crust of bread we had dropped on the ground. These scavengers, only an inch long, are born and grow up without a protective shell, and so for self-preservation they move—lock, stock and abdomen—into empty sea shells they find cast up on the beach. Threatened, a soldier crab pulls back into the shell it has appropriated, totally blocking the entrance with one big blue claw. But there is a flaw in the soldier crabs' unique adaptation: though they grow, their sea-shell houses do not. Thus growing crabs continually seek newer and larger quarters. Once on the Pacific coast of Panama a friend of mine

Teeth bared, a great barracuda about four feet long cruises past a grove of whiplike coral stalks. The largest of the 20 barracuda species, this silvery assassin depends on its coloring and slim body to help conceal it as it streaks after prey at speeds of up to 30 mph.

day. Indeed, in an experiment some years ago manatees from the Everglades were placed in certain northern Florida canals in the hope that their prodigious appetites could control the water hyacinths proliferating there. But before they could prove their worth on this mission they caught pneumonia in the unaccustomed cold and were sent home.

Historians surmise that the manatee may have been responsible for launching the myth of the alluring mermaid. According to this theory, early seamen saw a manatee use a flipper to hold her nursing pup to her breast, which mother manatees in fact do, and leaped to the conclusion that the creature they beheld was half woman, half fish. If this story is true, the sailors must have been at sea for a long time, since manatees, male or female, are among the homeliest creatures in creation. They have small eyes, thick lips, bristly muzzles and wrinkled necks. But unappealing as they may be to us, they certainly appeal to each other. Affectionate animals, they kiss each other, sometimes swim with linked flippers and always make solicitous parents.

Though manatees once ranged from South America up to North Carolina, today only a few remain in the most southerly waters of the United States, and not very many in Central America. Traditionally they have been hunted for their flesh, reputedly tender and delicious, and for their very tough hides, used in machine belting and high-pressure hoses. Now protected throughout Central America, they still suffer from collisions with powerboats in narrow creeks and canals.

Our own manatee was not about to collide with us, or even get close to us. We could tell where it was by the cloud of muddied water, but we could never see the animal itself. For about 15 minutes we followed the silty trail as the manatee moved on an erratic course through the lagoon, and although Willie spotted it once when it put its head up for a moment, it disappeared by the time I turned to look. Finally we could no longer see the trail—the manatee may have slipped into deeper water —and so we moved on across the lagoon. I confess I felt somewhat disappointed at missing the chance to see a mermaid in the flesh.

Toward evening Willie and I reached a pine ridge and set up camp for the night. A pine ridge in Belize is not really a ridge at all, but a broad savanna raised a few feet above the swamp streams. The jungle never got a toe hold on this poor, sandy soil. It is covered with low, tough, tussocky grass and here and there, standing in isolation, are Caribbean pines, twisted scrubs and occasional clumps of palmetto.

Willie had brought some turtle meat with him from Placentia, and

The waters around the cays and reefs off Central America's Caribbean coast provide these marine animals with easy living: warm subsurface temperatures that average about 80° F. and depths of less than 200 feet. All but one are sedentary creatures, feeding by filtering plankton from the water that swirls past them. The exception is the crinoid, which sometimes attaches itself to coral or rock but more often keeps on the move.

COLONIAL TUBE WORMS

FEATHER-STAR CRINOID

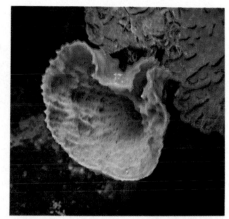

CHALICE SPONGE

FIRE CORAL

FINGER CORAL

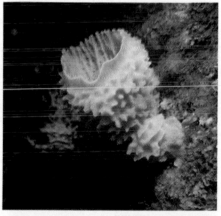

WHITE VASE SPONGE

PINK VASE SPONGE

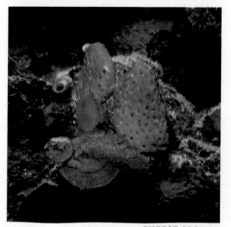

CHEESE SPONGE

APARTMENT SPONGE

while he built a fire and began to prepare a pot of stew, I got my binoculars and went for a stroll. There was an unexpected mood to the savanna. The openness of the country, the individual trees silhouetted against the horizon, the yellowing grass—these did not seem Central American at all. I half expected to see a pride of lions stalk from cover, or a herd of zebras on the distant plain. There are in fact animals around the pine ridge—particularly deer, both the whitetail and the brocket, the little red jungle deer that Belizeans call an antelope. I saw no deer, but I did catch out of the corner of my eye a flicker of brilliant red. When I lifted my glasses I saw a small bird, breathtaking in its brightness, lance out from a pine branch to snare an insect mid-air, then return to its perch. I had never seen this species before, but I recognized it immediately—a vermilion flycatcher, surely one of the most stunning small birds in Central America.

Pleased at having found a new bird to add to my list, I went back to the campfire. Sunset was coming on. From Willie's pot there came a savory smell of simmering sea turtle; the odor mingled with the unexpected scent of pitch from the pine knots in the fire. I tried to get Willie talking. He is shy around outsiders and taciturn at best, but once started he is well worth listening to. I began to ask questions about this and that, and after a while knowledge started spilling out, the stored-up wisdom of a lifelong woodsman and seaman.

When the wind comes from the north that's always bad on this coast. If the wind blows from the southeast that's bad too, because it's blowing against a norther that's moving down. Sometimes there's bad weather before a hurricane, but sometimes it's bell clear. The fish don't feed at dead low tide but they feed well when the tide starts coming in, then stop for an hour, then start feeding till high tide, when they go quiet again. When you gaff a strong fish, try to get him near the head so he can't twist around and chop at you.

Willie told some stories, too. About the time he was spear fishing and just grazed a barracuda with his spear, knocking some scales off, and the barra turned and came at him and he had to fend off the fish with his flippers. How as a boy he used to go out on the reef at the start of Lent, when there was the usual great demand for fish, and stay out with the fishermen for 40 days and nights. They slept in their boats or on little stilt-legged platforms built above the water, and he would wake every morning at four o'clock when the Caribs started blowing their conch-shell trumpets all up and down the reef.

Then there was the time Willie went hunting on a jungly cay; when he got back with two dead crocodiles to where he had anchored his boat, he found that it had washed away on the tide. He left his rifle and the crocodiles on the cay, and swam fully clothed for three and a half hours to the mainland. He was concerned only about sharks and the possibility of a cramp, since he knew he could swim from dawn to dark if he had to—it was no big thing, mon. On the mainland he found his dory, but the motor had torn loose and he had to dive to get it out of the mud. He cleaned it with gasoline from his fuel can, got it started and went straight back to collect his crocodiles; they were big ones and he had no intention of losing them.

As we talked it had grown dark. Up in the night sky the wide-mouthed birds known as pauraques were flying, their sad calls floating down soft as feathers. "We call that bird a who-you, because of its call," Willie said. "We've got a saying here, that if you pick up a who-you egg you can never put it down, because the shell is so thin it will break. So if somebody is in a ticklish situation, like maybe in a relationship with a woman, we say he's picked up a who-you egg."

Willie lifted the lid of the pot and stirred ambrosial odors out of the stew. "What kind of turtle is that, Willie?" I asked.

"Hawksbill," he said.

I winced. The hawksbill is a threatened species that sorely needs a respite from hunters. But there it was, in the pot, and there I was, ravenous. Was I a conservationist, or was I not? Willie dished up some stew and passed it over. I stared at it a moment. Then I began to eat.

Sea turtles are among the most extraordinary and mysterious of the creatures of the coastal country. Four species occur in the Caribbean, all of them large. Hatching from eggs the size of golf balls, the turtles mature to weights of from 125 pounds for the hawksbill, to 200 or 250 for the loggerhead and the green, on up to as much as 1,500 pounds for the leatherback. All sea turtles are great travelers, but the green turtles in particular accomplish incredible feats of long-range navigation. Each year between 3,000 and 8,000 of them make their way across hundreds and even thousands of miles of open sea to their only remaining major nesting site in the western Caribbean, a strip of Costa Rican beach at a place called Tortuguero. Only recently has it been discovered where newly hatched turtles go when they waddle into the sea and disappear. The baby turtles, from eight months to two years old, hitch rides to the shallow offshore waters of distant shores on sargassum rafts—drifting mats of floating algae. After reaching maturity there, they begin their long journeys back to the nesting ground, arriving as mature adults around 25 years later.

It is known that adult green turtles are chiefly herbivorous, the only large animals to dine at the Caribbean's vast banquet table of aquatic grasses. These turtle-grass pastures are found in abundance in the waters off the Central American coast. Out around the cays with Willie, I had seen acres and acres of such underwater meadows, the foot-long blades waving in the current like wheat before the wind. "A hundred years ago," one scientist had told me, "the turtles were so numerous in the Caribbean that they represented a food resource something on the order of the bison of the Plains in the Nineteenth Century. If the turtles were still here in their original numbers they could provide protein for the entire coastal population of Central America."

But the sea turtles were too succulent for their own good. The Indians netted and harpooned them. To have a continuous supply of fresh meat on voyages, buccaneers and merchantmen captured turtles alive and stored them, upside down, on the decks of their ships. The major threat to the turtle population, however, came on nesting beaches like Tortuguero. At night, during the nesting season, "turtle turners" patrolled the beaches, wrestling the armored creatures onto their backs, where they lay helplessly until boats picked them up the following day.

The eggs, too, were vulnerable. Coatimundis, raccoons, vultures and dogs dug up the nests and helped themselves. So did human beings. Some believed the eggs could cure impotence; everyone knew they were delicious.

By the mid-20th Century several sea-turtle species, including the green turtle, were threatened with extinction. Fortunately, during the 1950s the Tortuguero nesting colony was discovered by biologist-writer Archie Carr. A lifelong student of sea turtles, Carr enlisted sympathy for them with his eloquent writing, and along with influential friends formed a kind of international lobby. The lobby—originally called the Brotherhood of the Green Turtle—worked with the Costa Rican government to establish Tortuguero as a sanctuary where the turtles could nest unmolested and later provided funds for a research station.

In October, a few months before my camping trip with Willie Faux in Belize, I had flown to Tortuguero in a light plane to learn something of the turtles. We landed on a long, narrow strip of beach that lay between the sea and a lagoon bordered by coconut and raffia palms. At the research station tucked among the palm trees, I met Chuck Carr, Ar-

A slender coconut palm and a bushy cluster of red mangrove trees share the leeward side of a cay off Belize. The seeds of both species can endure long periods of immersion in salt water and still retain their ability to germinate.

chie's son and a biologist in his own right. "The nesting season is over," Chuck said, "but you should see some hatchlings." Out under the sand, along 20 miles of beach, the turtle eggs were just ready to hatch. More than 700 turtles had been tagged, nesting on the five-mile strip of beach patrolled by the people at the research station; even greater numbers had nested on another 15 miles of beach stretching to the south. Each female had dug three or four egg chambers during the season, depositing about a hundred eggs in each one. Chuck calculated mentally, then said, "This year there were probably 800,000 eggs laid on the beach."

I did some calculating myself. Figuring a sizable adult as weighing about 250 pounds, that meant something like *100,000 tons* of potential green turtle were out there under the sand. But Chuck warned me not to be misled. Newly hatched turtles are bite sized, soft shelled and prey to everything with claws, beaks or fins. Only the lucky ones survive.

It is not always easy to see baby sea turtles. After hatching, the youngsters usually wait beneath the surface of the sand until nightfall or dawn; then, while the darkness conceals them, they come to the surface and break for the sea. However, for observation purposes a few nests near the station had been surrounded by wire mesh. One morning Chuck asked, "How'd you like to let some baby turtles go?"

Down the beach, inside a wire enclosure, 100 little turtles were waving their flippers and clambering over their fellow hatchlings' backs, eager to be off on their journey to God-knows-where. I picked one of them up and looked at it. Sea turtles would win no beauty contests, but there was something irresistible about this creature. It had a neat gray carapace, and a beaked head with heavy-lidded eyes. The shell was soft and leathery, and even as I held the turtle in my hands its little flippers were paddling furiously, for the swim frenzy was already upon it. Programed to travel fast and steadily in order to escape the hungry mouths that await them, baby sea turtles are in continuous motion from the time they reach the surface of the sand and head for the sea; for their first few days in the water they do nothing but swim frantically.

"Any frigate birds around?" Chuck asked, scanning the sky for the predators. The coast clear, he lifted the edge of the wire mesh. Instantly the mass of turtles separated into scurrying individuals. They moved as jerkily as windup toys but headed purposefully for the surf. "There they go," Chuck grinned. "A hundred little walking machines."

Some turtles went straight and fast toward the sea. Others plowed off in the wrong direction; then, aware that something was wrong, they stopped, looked about and reaimed themselves. Some fell into footprints or pockets in the sand, or blundered into driftwood. But their tiny flippers kept windmilling away, and aimless as their flailing seemed they soon got over or under or around the obstacles and hurried on.

One hatchling got hung up behind a big driftwood log and tried to climb over it, without success. The turtle turned off and moved laterally, then tried to climb the log again. In the normal course of events it might eventually have got around the log; more likely a predator would have snapped it up, or the hot sun would have baked it to death. Without feeling the least bit hesitant about interfering with the processes of nature, I picked up the turtle and set it down on the other side of the log, where it immediately started propelling itself seaward again, without so much as a backward glance at the *deus ex machina* who had just saved it from an unpleasant fate.

I walked down toward the water. The first hatchlings had just reached the last slope to the water's edge; the surf lay only a few feet away. My turtle paused at the top of the slope for a moment and surveyed the sea that would be home for the rest of its life. The world out there was full of terrifying things: hungry jacks and mackerel and barracuda patrolling just offshore; gulls and terns and frigate birds with penetrating eyes and fierce beaks; and later, if the turtle survived and grew large and strong, men would be waiting with harpoons and nets. The very thought of all those hazards would be enough to paralyze a grown man with fright. But there is a kind of wonderful, blind bravery in small creatures, and I suppose that is why nature is so resilient.

After a moment the little turtle plunged on down the sandy slope and into the first breaker, flippers flailing furiously. The wave threw the hatchling back up onto the beach, but the flippers never stopped, and the second wave lifted the turtle, splashed over it and carried it out. A tiny ball of living stuff, disappearing in the crest of each wave but always reemerging beyond, it swam steadily toward the open sea.

I watched until it was out of sight, and even then the image lingered in my mind. Four months later, as I sat on the pine ridge in Belize with Willie Faux, guiltily enjoying my plate of hawksbill stew, I thought of the hatchling I had helped on its first steps seaward, and I hoped that unlike the hawksbill, it had so far avoided becoming something's dinner.

The Treasure of Tortuguero

The coastal enclave called Tortuguero, stretching along the Caribbean shore of Costa Rica, is unique among Central America's wild places. Within it are four distinct habitats, each with its own character, plants and creatures—though the latter tend to range across natural boundaries to prey on one another. Fronting on the sea is an expanse of sand beach (right). Behind that is a narrow lagoon, connected to the sea at one end and fed by a river at the other. Back of the lagoon is a coastal rain forest threaded by serpentine streams; and on the periphery of the forest lies a complex of swamps.

This formidable topography has helped make Tortuguero almost impregnable to human assault. The winding inland waterways have stymied would-be road builders. Logging on a large scale has also been futile; the high salt content of the rain forest's soil and air has prevented the growth of marketable trees such as mahogany and rubber. At the sea's edge a safe anchorage is denied to marine traffic by strong coastal currents and onshore winds as well as by the lack of protective banks or reefs.

Only small boats can approach the beach, and indeed, they came here for years, carrying market hunters who raided Tortuguero's chief natural treasure—the legions of large green sea turtles that use the beach as a nesting ground. But in 1965 the Costa Rican government declared Tortuguero off limits to turtle hunters and designated its 22 miles of beach, as well as some portions of the adjoining habitats, as a national park. Thus protected, the turtles, which had been dangerously depleted, can breed undisturbed by man and thus restore their numbers. Each year from May to October, fleets of adult hawksbill, leatherback and green turtles return from their ocean travels to mate offshore and nest on the beach (pages 146-147).

The only peril these species still face on land is an age-old one: fellow creatures such as coatimundis, ocelots and peccaries emerge from the rain forest to dig up new-laid turtle eggs or to pounce on hatchlings making their way seaward.

But these deadly encounters are just one part of the grand design that nature has imposed on the rich and varied habitats of Tortuguero, where each form of life, animal or plant, is free to work out its own modus vivendi and to seek a special niche in which it can effectively survive.

Foamy Caribbean rollers fan out on Tortuguero's beach. Though the sand was black when this picture was taken, at other times it changes to a light gray. This phenomenon results from the fact that the beach is composed of two kinds of volcanic particles, pumice and obsidian, washed down from two ancient, eroding volcanoes some 40 miles inland. Depending on the strength and direction of waves and wind, either the light-colored pumice or the darker obsidian shows on top.

Seen from a low hill on the jungle's edge, Tortuguero's lagoon parallels the beach for its full, 22-mile length. The lagoon's brackish waters are fed both by the Caribbean breaching the sand barrier at the left, and by jungle streams looping in at the far right.

A corner of the rain forest (right) combines the elements of habitat that support the majority of Tortuguero's jungle creatures. Profuse plant growth provides food and cover for animals like those shown here—and soaks up ground water so rapidly that even torrential rains do not cause the streams to rise more than two inches.

A long-nosed coatimundi snuffles along a branch in a leisurely search for a meal.

On a rare visit to the forest floor, a tree-dwelling iguana scurries to seek cover.

A surly eyed three-toed sloth rests in its descent of a strangler fig tree.

Black stingless bees gather pollen on the coblike flower (above) of a bactris palm. If another bee tries to move in on their territory, the stingless bees emit sticky substances that allow them to seize an invader in flight and bring it down by weight of numbers.

The so-called stilt roots of a socratea palm (left) prop up a central trunk that is less than six inches in diameter although some 50 feet tall. The underground portion of this complex tree's root system is very shallow, and the stilts provide an anchor for the palm in the rain-forest soil.

The delicate, multicolored blossom of the moisture-loving Odoratissimum cochliostema (right), less formally called the commelina, emerges from among the stiff green leaves that make up a protective sheathing.

A young geonomoid palm fans out its elegantly striped leaves. The red tint, common to new leaves of jungle plants, comes from a pigment that blocks the sun's ultraviolet rays and keeps new tissue from burning up until a chlorophyll layer develops.

The winding *Río Palacio* creates a broad opening in the rain forest as it moves toward a swampy area behind Tortuguero beach. Exposed to the sun, the riverside vines grow more densely than the shaded vines deep in the forest, and they cover their host trees with thick cascades of greenery.

A boat-billed heron (above) scans the jungle with bulbous eyes so keenly light sensitive that the bird can spot and scoop up small fish and frogs from the water in the dead of night.

A red-eyed tree frog (below) balances on long hind legs, ready to leap at any passing insect. The frog catches its prey in mid-air; suction disks on its toes guarantee a sure-footed landing.

Broad-leafed calathea and fernlike raffia, two of

the more than 20 species of palm that flourish throughout the inland habitats of Tortuguero, throng the margins of a sluggish watercourse.

Her egg-laying mission accomplished the previous night, a green turtle (left) furrows a path across Tortuguero's beach as she makes her way back to the sea to resume her life in the water.

A hefty leatherback (right) tests the Caribbean surf. Largest of all sea turtles, leatherbacks average 800 pounds in weight, and some specimens may grow to a length of seven feet.

A hawksbill turtle (below) reconnoiters the beach. Of the three species on Tortuguero, the hawksbill makes the fastest work of the nesting process: in less than two hours it digs a shallow pit, lays up to 160 eggs, and departs.

The ground-hugging beach morning-glory brightly carpets part of Tortuguero's shore. A rapid grower—12 inches long only a month after

The P
erers, w
and col
gum. B
begun t
been br
cluding
area; oi
limesto
vades t
raw and

From
across t
ny dogs
with a
Sam Hil
jungle.
hands.
now the
our que
we pick
much r
and the
push bu

The r
hired fo
into the
the tow
that the
long tri
a very
day. Th
drums
and Sa
canoa,
hot; Co
in a fe
cooled

The I
to follo

germination—it is also the most heat resistant and salt tolerant of all plants, helping stabilize the sand and prepare it for other plants.

gether they form the big, northward-flowing Río Usumacinta, which ultimately ends in the Gulf of Mexico. Here, however, it forms the international boundary between Guatemala and Mexico, and we wanted to see at least part of it after we had traveled the Pasión.

Just below Sayaxché, the Pasión broadened, still moving slowly. The only sign of man was an occasional thatch-roofed hut in a burned-over field, although the jungle alongside the café-au-lait water had a stunted look, as if it had been logged at some time in the past.

Snowy egrets fished along the banks, brilliant white against the brilliant green of the foliage, and large, ridge-backed turtles slid off logs as we approached. Iguanas six feet long basked in the sun on branches that hung over the water. From time to time Manuel slowed the boat to point out one of these enormous lizards, but at first Co and I could never see the creature until it launched itself out over the bushes and crashed into the water below. This behavior is characteristic, for while the iguanas of Central America are tree dwellers, they are also excellent swimmers and divers, and will nearly always choose the water as an escape route when they feel threatened. Indeed, the 16th Century historian Oviedo y Valdés could not decide whether iguanas were "beastes of the lande or fyshes, because they lyve in the water, and wander in the woddes and on the lande."

I finally fixed an iguana in my binoculars before it plunged from its perch. Magnified by nine, it was a reptilian nightmare, a living relic from the dinosaur age. The iguana's head, the size of a large fist, was crested with a fright wig of leathery spikes. Its heavy body was encased in a scaly hide that drooped in deep wrinkles around the sockets of muscular legs. Yet for all its menacing appearance the iguana is quite harmless, a nonbelligerent vegetarian. This one, concluding that *we* were the sinister presence on the river, scuttled from its branch and dived into the water with a huge splash.

In midafternoon we reached the place we had chosen for our first night's camp—an abandoned archeological site known as Altar de los Sacrificios. On the riverbank were two half-collapsed thatched huts, perhaps the quarters of the archeologists who had studied the site decades ago. Behind the huts the jungle closed in tightly. There was no trail that I could discern, but Manuel confidently unsheathed his machete and began to hack his way into the wall of greenery.

In the stillness of the rain forest the machete rang like a bell as it sliced through lianas and palm fronds. Finally Manuel stopped and slashed at the grasses and low brush at his feet. In a moment he had exposed two great steles lying flat on the ground. These stone slabs had been carved by the Maya as monuments to their leaders. The larger was perhaps eight feet long by five feet wide and two feet thick; it must have weighed several tons. On its face, very faint, was the pattern of Maya glyphs. They were indecipherable to me, of course, but probably they recorded the monument's date and the name of the man to whose memory it had been erected, along with his rank, honorific titles and achievements.

We moved on, following more trails only Manuel could see, to other fallen monuments, all hidden in the undergrowth until the quick, bright blade of the machete revealed them. Huge and blackened by time, crumbled and broken, invaded by mosses and lichens, their inscriptions eroded until scarcely visible, the monuments lay everywhere, their worn glyphs singing the praises of long-departed leaders only to the ocean of greenery that enveloped them.

On top of a ridge we came to a beautiful spot where corozo palms shot their fronds skyward in long, graceful curves to form a vaulted, sun-dappled ceiling. In the middle of the grove Manuel's blade flashed again, and there was the sacrificial altar, a wheel of stone perhaps six feet across, perfectly round, covered with a layer of soft green moss. Whether human lives were actually taken on this particular altar no one knows. But the Maya lived in a hard country, and they felt a constant need to propitiate the gods with sacrifice and self-mutilation. They pierced their tongues and penises with sting-ray spines, and lopped off heads or chopped out hearts on the steps of their temples or on altars like this one. Beneath the arched ceiling of palms, the round stone seemed almost a part of the jungle itself, but somehow sinister too—a durable reminder of man's willingness to destroy his own kind.

Later, back at the riverbank, Co went with Manuel to try to photograph iguanas, while Salvador helped me set up the new tent I had bought, one made specially for camping in the tropics. It proved to be a complicated device with an inner envelope of mosquito netting and a separate waterproof fly, each of which had to be guyed separately. After 20 minutes I began to feel the need of a civil engineer's assistance. Shrouded in mosquitoes, I crouched in the long grass with sweat pouring down my back and wrestled with a spider's web of nylon lines. It took another 15 minutes to get the confounded thing up, and the fly taut and even. Salvador grinned at me. "Una carpa bonita," he said. A pretty tent. It was indeed pretty now that it was erected—a nice blue

color, light and airy, as elegant in its lines as the Golden Gate Bridge.

Salvador went off to start a cooking fire while I watched dusk coming to the river and the jungle. A cooling breeze had sprung up. The mournful calls of tinamous rang from the forest and the rich smells of the jungle lay thick in my nostrils.

Across the river the sun's last rays illuminated the crown of a colossal ceiba that stood 50 feet higher than the rest of the forest canopy. The lesser trees were already blue with dusk, but the ceiba was touched by fire, like a mountain bathed in alpenglow. For me, the ceiba is the most beautiful tree of the American tropics. Its massive gray-green trunk shoots clean and straight and branchless for 100 feet into the air, and terminates in a crown that mushrooms above the other trees. From a plane the crowns look like islands in the sea; from the ground the ceiba is just as impressive. In a forest in Panama I had seen one so gigantic that as I approached, its buttressed trunk looked like a great gray building emerging from the trees. Standing within the amphitheater of its roots, I realized that this was a tree I had envisioned as a child, the tree in which the Swiss Family Robinson had made its home. The Maya had believed that the world was supported by four giant ceibas; now, watching the sunset on the tree across the river, that belief seemed not fanciful at all.

The light faded. A pair of macaws, screeching, flew across the river, long tails dragging behind. The sky in the quarter opposite the sun glowed pink, hummed with a kind of incandescence. An ant shrike called from the forest. In a few minutes it was dark.

At night in the Pretty Tent, with the mosquitoes snarling like Messerschmitts on the other side of the netting, sleep was difficult. So I lay in the darkness and thought of the altar I had seen earlier in the day and the stone slabs now fallen and overgrown by jungle. Precisely when the first Maya came to the Petén is uncertain, but by around 300 A.D. they had begun to master the region. They transformed patches of the jungle into cornfields; they built splendid cities and temples whose relics still stagger the imagination, and they developed sophisticated arts and mathematics and an extraordinary culture that lasted for 600 years. Then, in the Ninth Century A.D., they vanished virtually overnight.

No one knows why the Maya civilization ended so abruptly. A traditional theory has been that the slash-and-burn agriculture practiced by the Maya totally changed the environment of the Petén. Then as now, farmers could get only two or three harvests from a patch of

The still surface of the Río de la Pasión reflects a mirrored image of fleecy cumulus clouds and vine-clad trees along the riverbanks.

burned-off jungle before indestructible weeds took over. They had to move on to a new piece of land and let the old fields lie fallow for about 10 years, by which time the forest had grown enough to shade out the weeds; then the Maya would slash and burn again. As they increased in numbers they simply ran out of jungle to burn, and eventually turned the whole region into an untillable savanna.

To someone with an ecological set of mind this may be a satisfying explanation for the disappearance of the Maya, but today most scientists find it unconvincing. Some archeologists have advanced other explanations—epidemic disease, earthquake, even drought. Still another theory is that the common people simply got sick and tired of the many burdens imposed upon them, including the hauling of all those heavy rocks for the deification of their leaders, and so they toppled their own civilization through social revolution.

This last idea seemed plausible to me. At Tikal, 78 miles northeast across the Petén, I had walked among the magnificently restored Maya temples, my mind filled with visions of panoply and splendor: of priests robed in the skins of jaguars and the feathers of macaws and quetzals; of noblemen being carried majestically above the heads of the multitudes through spacious plazas that echoed with the roll of drums and strident blasts on conch-shell trumpets. But the great civilizations were often great only for a few, and here, at this forgotten site in the jungle, with its monuments crumbling and moldering away, the vision was different. As I lay in the tent I saw in my mind's eye the blood of sacrifice on the moss-covered altar, saw the knotted leg muscles and the bowed, straining backs, the sweat and the grimaces of pain, as the Maya moved the great stones, God knows how, to their resting places in the jungle.

In the morning we continued down the Pasión to its confluence with the Río Salinas, where the two rivers boil together to form the Río Usumacinta. Measured along its sinuous bends, the Usumacinta flows for almost 300 miles. In the past it has been a route down which timber cutters have floated logs of mahogany, the most valuable wood in the Petén. Mahogany not only is beautifully grained but is of such close texture that it can be cut into sheets of veneer only 1/85 of an inch thick. The trees have been avidly sought for centuries, and since they are widely dispersed in the forest, oldtime loggers employed spotters who climbed high into the canopy to scan the surrounding jungle for the mahogany's distinctive spreading crown of dark-green, leathery leaves. More recently, airplane spotters have filled the same function, but today little mahogany cutting takes place because the trees have been virtually wiped out.

We headed down the Usumacinta, with Mexico to our left, Guatemala to our right. After about six miles Manuel nosed the skiff into the brush-hidden mouth of a tributary stream on the Guatemalan side, which he said led to a lake called Laguna Ixcoche. The stream was small and overhung with trees, and so serpentine that Salvador, behind us in the long *canoa,* had difficulty negotiating the bends. At our approach big ringed kingfishers rattled off into the forest; every so often tiny green kingfishers paced the boat. After a while there was a lightening in the trees ahead, and we came out into Ixcoche.

For the next couple of hours we explored the lake. It was long and narrow, the water dark and smooth as glass. The jungle along the shores right here had never seen an ax or saw, and the ceibas and the pale-barked, ghostly fig trees called *chimones* lifted their crowns high above an understory of corozo palms. Ixcoche lay in an arc two or three miles long. It was obviously what geologists call an oxbow lake. At one time it had been a bend of the Usumacinta, but long ago the river had shortened itself, cutting across the neck of the bend and leaving its former channel to lie as a peaceful, quiet lake.

Accessible only by the half-hidden stream that joined it to the Usumacinta, the lake had escaped human impact. There were no buildings, no sign of man whatsoever. Macaws called from the jungle canopy. In a marshy area near the far end a billow of huge Muscovy ducks with white flashes in their wings went up at our approach. Along the banks schools of fish were on the move, their fins slicing the water.

We set up camp in a cool and lovely grove of corozo palms on the lake shore. Co and I erected the Pretty Tent, then went to see what Manuel and Salvador were up to. With their machetes they had already built three *champas,* simple but effective shelters made from overlapping corozo fronds. The fronds are actually immense leaves, the biggest 16 to 19 feet long, with a tough texture that makes them impervious to the heaviest rain. One of the *champas* Manuel and Salvador erected was for cooking, and in the other two they were arranging their own sleeping quarters. I had brought with me a big frame backpack stuffed with the most up-to-date, scientifically designed camping equipment in existence—several hundred dollars' worth of ripstop nylon, ultra-light alloys and space-age engineering. Manuel and Salvador had brought only their machetes and cloth bags containing their simple hammocks and muslin mosquito nets. Yet it was clear now, looking at the camp they had made within a few minutes, that they were going to be every bit as comfortable as I was; perhaps more so.

Back out on the lake, we explored the shoreline and I tried a bit of fishing. Fish were rolling close to shore, and although they showed no interest in my plugs, I accidentally foul hooked one. It looked like a blue catfish of only a couple of pounds, and I was disappointed, but Manuel smiled. "Deleeshus," he said, and whopped it on the head.

As we drifted in the boat, the sunset that spread over Ixcoche was superlative even by tropical standards. We watched as the anvil clouds caught fire and burned. Far down the lake we could see the silver slashes of rolling tarpon; at this point they were about 250 miles up the Usumacinta from their other home in the salt water of the Gulf of Mexico. Then from the jungle came a screeching and screaming that grew louder and louder, and in a moment a flock of macaws appeared above the tallest trees. There must have been 60 of them, flying in such tight pairs that each pair seemed a single bird with two sets of wings and a long tandem tail. Flamboyant against the sunset clouds, they crossed the lake and disappeared into the darkening jungle on the other side.

What magnificent creatures these giant parrots are; how arrogant! No protective coloration for the macaws. No creeping quietly around trying to blend in with the country and hoping to be overlooked. Scarlet and blue and gold, their colors are so bright you can hardly look at them without squinting, and their voices are so loud and filled with authority they seem ready to challenge all creation. Even when moving from branch to branch in the trees they seem swaggering and prideful as emperors. Their huge hooked beaks are so powerful they could sever a man's finger, and it is hard to imagine a macaw fearing anything. I would not be surprised to see one strut up to a jaguar, utter a single imperious squawk, and send the fellow on his way. Yet macaws can be quite touching in their affection for each other. They live to be very old —50 years or more—and are believed to mate for life. One rarely sees a macaw alone; they are almost always paired, male and female often sitting side by side, grooming and preening each other and conversing in rasping but loving tones; or they will be flying, as we had just seen them, two by two.

At night the catfish I had hooked, now gutted and spitted on a sharp stick, roasted slowly over the coals. As we started to eat, we heard a faint rustling in the trees not far away. Quickly Manuel blew out our candle. "Mico de noche," he whispered—night monkey.

I knew he meant what we call a kinkajou—not a monkey at all, but a

In a Guatemalan rain forest a young-adult kinkajou—relative of the raccoon and the panda—uses its prehensile tail and the sharp, curved claws of its hind feet to keep a grip on a branch.

close relative of the raccoon. Manuel began to suck at the back of his hand, producing a loud squeaking noise. In a moment there was more rustling in the trees, then silence. I very much hoped to see the animal, for kinkajous are charming creatures. Their coats are golden brown and velvet soft, and since they are totally nocturnal they have large limpid eyes. They also have muscular two-foot-long bodies and only slightly shorter prehensile tails that make them superb climbers, and they spend virtually their entire lives in treetops, feeding on fruit, honey and insects. At night they are hyperactive, and in the daytime very drowsy; if you pick up a tame kinkajou in the daylight hours, its first instinct is to cuddle against your chest, bury its head so the light doesn't hurt its eyes, and drop off to sleep.

Manuel squeaked again, and now we could hear the kinkajou moving slowly toward us through the trees. Sitting in the darkness with only the faintest illumination from the embers of the campfire, I felt pleasantly spooky, as if all my senses were in touch with the jungle.

Suddenly, directly overhead, there was a sharp, explosive cry. The animal was right there, almost on top of us. We all simultaneously switched on our flashlights and probed them into the roof of the jungle. Scanning, we picked apart the foliage with our flashlight beams, expecting to catch the gleam of the kinkajou's eyes. But we could see nothing, only the illuminated green of the leaves.

In the morning, I itched in a way I have never itched in my life. In spite of the Pretty Tent the mosquitoes had managed to get to me, and so had some chiggers and the flies Sam Hill had warned us about back in Sayaxché. Co had gone off with Manuel to take pictures. I told Salvador desperately, "Listen, I'm going crazy, I've got to take a bath." He stared, not understanding my English. I had forgotten the Spanish for bath. I pointed at myself and said "Lavandería," which means laundry, but that was close enough. Salvador grinned and nodded.

We took the *canoa* to a sand bar in the middle of the lake. I ripped off my clothes, jumped into the water and sighed with pure pleasure. I spent half an hour washing in waist-deep water, while little fish nibbled at my legs and the Wilson's plovers on the sand bar eyed me curiously. By the time I finished, I once again loved my fellow man.

Afterward we explored a stream that flowed into the lake. Salvador paddled the *canoa* along it slowly, snaking the boat expertly through tangles of fallen logs. As we rounded a bend he hissed at me and pointed toward the bank ahead. "*Brazo fuerte,*" he whispered. I knew that

A normally nocturnal tayra prowls through a Central American jungle on an overcast morning. One of the biggest members of the weasel family, weighing up to 10 pounds, the tayra habitually preys on tree squirrels and other rodents but has been known to make quick work of small deer.

meant strong arm, but I had no idea what sort of beast the name sig-
nified. It took me a couple of minutes to spot the animal, low and
sinuous, its body dark, shading to blond on the neck and head.

Including the tail, the creature was about three feet long. As it stood
on a length of fallen bamboo it began to move its head in a peculiar bobbing and weaving motion. I realized that it was a weasel of some kind,
although an enormous one. I mentally sorted through my reading and
in a moment I knew what it was: a tayra, the big weasel of Central and
South America. Tayras are strong enough to pull down and kill the
young brocket deer of the lowland forests. They have a reputation for
being fearless—a characteristic they share with other members of their
tribe—and indeed the one on the bank seemed not in the least fright-
ened. It watched closely as we drifted nearer, and it continued that bobbing and weaving motion of its head and neck. Why weasels do that I
don't know; one theory holds that with their small heads and close-set
eyes, they have poor depth perception, and so compensate by making
these odd movements. In any case, there is something a little scary
about the sight; I always get the feeling that the weasel is sizing me up
to see what kind of meal I would make.

Never taking its gaze off us, the tayra let us float by. At a distance of
no more than 20 feet, I could see that its eyes were dark and lustrous,
its ears neat and set on a triangular, serpent-like head. After we got
past, I looked back. The tayra poked around on the bank for a moment
more, then disappeared into the jungle with a motion so fluid that it
seemed to flow over the earth like a snake.

When we went back to camp for lunch, I picked up a corozo-palm
nut from the ground and asked Salvador if it was good to eat. "Sí,
buena," he replied, and with his machete he opened the nut for me. It
was sweet and pleasant to the taste, but the real pleasure was in watching Salvador open it. Observing a Guatemalan woodsman use a machete
is almost an esthetic experience. Every Guatemalan male seems to have
come into the world equipped with two arms, two legs and one machete. The machete is always on his person, either held in his hand or
sheathed in his belt, except when he is in church and, presumably,
when in bed. When he is not cutting something with his machete, he is
sharpening it. He uses it as a knife, a can opener, an ax, a hammer, a
scythe and occasionally as a weapon, and it would not surprise me in
the least to see a Guatemalan shave with a machete.

Had I been trying to open that palm nut with a machete I suppose I
could have, at considerable risk to my fingers—but with nothing like

Salvador's virtuosity and elegance. This is how he did it: first, with four sharp chops, he cut a flat notch out of a tree root, thus making a chopping block. Next, with two surgically precise blows, he shaved off one end of the nut, then the other. He now had a nut that was roughly spherical, but flattened on both ends. He then stood the nut on one flat end on the chopping block, raised the machete, and split the nut exactly in half with a single blow.

In the afternoon the two of us took the *canoa* out to the Río Usumacinta to see if we could buy tortillas from a farmer. A few miles upstream we pulled up to the muddy bank next to a crude thatch-palm hut, occupied by a family that had been relocated to the Petén by the Guatemalan government as part of a program to reduce the population pressure on the highlands. The children were ragged and dirty and had bad skin infections; the farmer himself had an eye almost closed by an angry sty. On a bench in front of the hut sprawled a dead spider monkey, recently shot. Its arms were wrapped around an empty rum bottle and its head was tilted to one side as if drunk—the mordant humor of people who live a hard life.

While Salvador tried to buy the tortillas I walked around behind the hut to the edge of a new clearing a couple of acres in size. The land looked as though an artillery barrage had fallen there, leaving behind a tangle of half-burned stumps and fallen tree trunks. But in the spaces between the trunks, bright green shoots of young corn were thrusting up. The clearing was typical of the slash-and-burn agriculture that is found all across the Petén, and indeed across a large part of Central America—the same kind of agriculture practiced by the Maya. When carried on by Indians it had been a reasonably sound form of land stewardship, since the tillers moved on to new land and the jungle reclaimed the old, unused fields. But today, with the rise in population and a new practice of pasturing cattle on the land once the initial crops have been harvested, the slash-and-burn technique is using up land at a fearsome rate. No one could deny the wretched family on the Usumacinta the right to wrest whatever poor living they can from the thin jungle soil. What is fortunate, however, is that in recent years Central American governments have ordered some of the undeveloped areas to be set aside as parks or multiple-use preserves.

By the time Salvador and I returned to our camp at the lake, I was in a surly mood, depressed at the utter poverty of the family I had met, yet angry at the thought of what the exigencies of modern life were doing to the jungle. The mood lasted well into the next day. I decided to try fishing, which is usually therapeutic for me, and Salvador and I went off in the *canoa*. For the next couple of hours I flogged the water, with no reaction except a couple of halfhearted strikes, which I missed.

Frustrated, I went back to camp. Manuel and Co, who had made their own trip out to the Usumacinta, had bought wild meat from a farmer there, and it was smoking over the fire. There were some strips of *jabalí*—the little forest pig we call javelina or peccary—and a chunk of *tepescuintle*. The *tepescuintle* is a giant, white-spotted nocturnal rodent that looks something like a cross between a guinea pig and a white-tailed fawn. All over Central America both two-legged and four-legged predators regard its flesh as a delicacy.

Late in the afternoon I heard Salvador calling from the lake. I went down to the shore to find him triumphantly holding up a basslike fish of about three pounds, which he had just caught on a hook baited with *tepescuintle* meat. I glared at the fish and at Salvador. I had brought enough fishing tackle to open my own sporting-goods store. Yet I had been shown up by the old barefoot-boy-with-pole-and-bent-pin routine —except that Salvador had not even had the grace to use a pole, just a length of line wrapped around his hand. "Okay," I said grimly. So we went back out on the lake and I pounded the water till my arm was sore. Finally, just as it was getting dark, I said, "Salvador, you win." I cut off my lure, tied on a naked hook, and handed it over so that Salvador could bait it with a piece of *tepescuintle* meat, while I sat in humiliation. On my first cast with the *tepescuintle* meat, I caught a fish.

At night we dined on roast *jabalí*, roast *tepescuintle* and my catch, a bluegill-like fish called a *mojarra*. After so sumptuous a meal I felt expansive, my surliness forgotten. Co, tired after a long day of taking pictures, went to bed. I stayed up talking with Manuel and Salvador. And there was something really exciting to talk about: Manuel had learned from a farmer on the Usumacinta that *el tigre*, the jaguar, had been seen that very day not far from where we were now camped.

To me, the jaguar is a symbol of the Central American jungles just as the wolf is a symbol of the far north. It is not only largest of the American cats, but also ranks with the African or Asian leopard as the largest of the world's spotted cats. A versatile hunter, at home in trees, on the ground and even in water, the jaguar is powerful enough to kill a full-grown cow, although it will also lie lazily on a riverbank, one paw dangling in the water, as it waits to flip out a passing fish or turtle. People who live on the forest borders fear *el tigre,* but in fact jaguars are extremely shy and not particularly dangerous. They are certainly strong enough to kill an unarmed human if they want to, but unlike their look-alikes, the leopards, they almost never become man-eaters.

Jaguars have become increasingly rare over their entire former range, both because their wild habitat has been destroyed and because they have been heavily hunted by sportsmen and local farmers. One man in our part of the Petén, Manuel said, had killed 10 jaguars in a single year, and now it was very unusual for anyone to see one of the big cats.

As Manuel talked, it occurred to me that he was voicing the same sad refrain I had been hearing, in musical Creole or fluid Spanish, all over Central America. Sea turtles getting scarce now. Lobsters getting scarce. Not much mahogany left. Yes, there are tapirs, but you don't often see one now. Similar lamentations, I suppose, would have been heard in the United States in the late 19th Century—in fact, they still are heard, from a few oldtime woodsmen. But in Central America one hears the sorry roll call of a disappearing heritage from people in their thirties, even in their twenties. In the United States, because of the efforts of a few far-seeing conservationists, some remarkably good decisions were made many decades ago, decisions that resulted in the saving of substantial pieces of the country's wilderness. In Central America the decisions are only now being made.

The task of convincing skeptical Central American governments that conservation makes good economic sense has taken years of effort by people like Dr. Gerardo Budowski, a Venezuelan agronomist who was the head of the prestigious International Union for the Conservation of Nature and Natural Resources. "The idea that conservation is a valid alternative for land use is almost unheard of here," he told me a few years ago. "The governments still view conservation as something of the rich and for the rich. The governments still want more roads, more farms, more development, even in the most fragile areas."

Yet for an outsider like me it is easy to sympathize with the dilemma that the Central Americans face. The republics are small, and poor, and desperately in need of economic development. Short-term gains loom large. Farming the jungle soil until the fertility gives out, then moving on, is cheaper than trying to keep one patch of land in production. In a time of high beef prices it is tempting to run cattle on land that is so steep or so fragile the soil will soon erode. And though it may be easy to pass laws for the protection of wildlife, where is the money to come from for enforcing the laws? When you don't have enough doctors and teachers, how can you afford a corps of government ecologists who fiddle about with an abstruse science, then tell you that you shouldn't be doing this or that? The economic value of a national park is hard to quantify and the pay-off is likely to be in the distant future. Besides, Central American governments have a wholly admirable aversion to making people pay admission to walk in the out-of-doors.

Yet partly because of the efforts of a growing number of Central American conservationists, partly as a result of the persuasive efforts of naturalists like Dr. Budowski and Anne LaBastille, there is a greater recognition of the environmental threat and a healthy regional movement to protect the choicer parts of the natural scene. National parks now exist in most Central American countries, and the number of protected areas increased from 23 to 160 between 1968 and 1981. Many more such areas are being surveyed and proposed. Additional areas may become multiple-use preserves. New laws in the United States and other nations now prohibit the import of products made from endangered species; these laws give a number of rare animals a chance at survival. While jaguars are still threatened, at least they are hunted less than they were a few years ago: fewer hunters want to risk the social disapproval that comes with killing a spotted cat, and fewer people want to be seen wearing its furs. The opportunities that remain for saving Central America's wild areas are good—if the present trend continues.

It was growing late at Ixcoche, and after a bit Manuel and Salvador went to their hammocks. I decided to sit up for a while and watch the firelight flickering on the trunks of the palms. My bites were not bothering me as much as they had, and I began to feel quite wonderful, that luxurious sensation one gets sometimes in the tropics in the shirtsleeve evening after the heat and sweat of the day.

Out beyond the firelight, perhaps not far from me, the jaguar Manuel had spoken of was moving carefully through the forest. I found that agreeable to contemplate. The big cat had managed to survive the bullets of hunters and the pressures of development and, for the moment anyway, we were able to share the same patch of jungle.

Back in the forest an owl began to call, a deep, resonant hooting that came from the direction of the Usumacinta. I stayed by the fire a little longer to listen, knowing that somewhere in the darkness the jaguar was listening too.

A Forest Brushed by Clouds

A dry day is so rare in the lofty forests of Guatemala's Sierra de las Minas that local people say the rainy season lasts for 13 months of the year. Warm, humid air blowing off the Caribbean is responsible, regularly climbing the range and bathing its cool green flanks in precipitation. Moisture-laden clouds drape the peaks like a delicate shawl, sending gauzy strands of mist through the trees. The perpetual wetness encourages riotous growth, notably of epiphytic plants, which draw much of their sustenance from the air. Some of them grow thicker than the trunks and branches of the white-pine, sweet-gum and avocado trees that serve as their hosts.

All these conditions are classic to what botanists label montane rain forest, more commonly called cloud forest. To the visitor the cloud forest seems a realm of fantasy seen through a succession of veils.

Co Rentmeester, who took the pictures that follow, is a veteran traveler familiar with the rain forests of Asia; yet the cloud forest of the Sierra de las Minas, 5,000 feet above sea level, had its own special fascinations for him.

The same elements that provided a wondrous spectacle for his cameras also presented problems during his forays into this high jungle from his base in the village of Purulhá on the northern flank of the range. A ceaseless drizzle forced him to rig up a small umbrella to shield his lenses. He had to use a machete to hack through the entangling growth—"a huge spaghetti pot of vines and leaves," he says. Once he had to work gingerly around a 150-foot-high roaring cataract (right).

But such vexations were forgotten in the otherworldly beauty of his surroundings. The sun did break through at rare moments, permitting photographs of such minutiae as waterdrops on horsetail (page 170). Most of the time, however, the forest was suffused by haze and shadow. The result was a moody, pastel quality that Rentmeester captured, for example, in his picture of a stand of sweet gums (pages 174-175). The views put him in mind of the canvases of the French painter Seurat, with their dots of color that fuse into a shimmering, soft-focus reality.

Fittingly, the clouds of the cloud forest proved most intriguing. Rentmeester found them "almost spooky. They float through the forest endlessly, flowing like an ocean of foam over a vast green shore."

TISATE BLOOMING BESIDE A CASCADE

WILD-AVOCADO TREE FESTOONED WITH RED EPIPHYTIC AIR PLANTS

MORNING DEW ON STALKS OF HORSETAIL

SAW-TOOTHED FURCREA LEAVES AND ENCROACHING VINE

WHITE PINE TOWERING INTO THE MIST

SUNSET OVER THE MOUNTAINS NEAR PURULHA

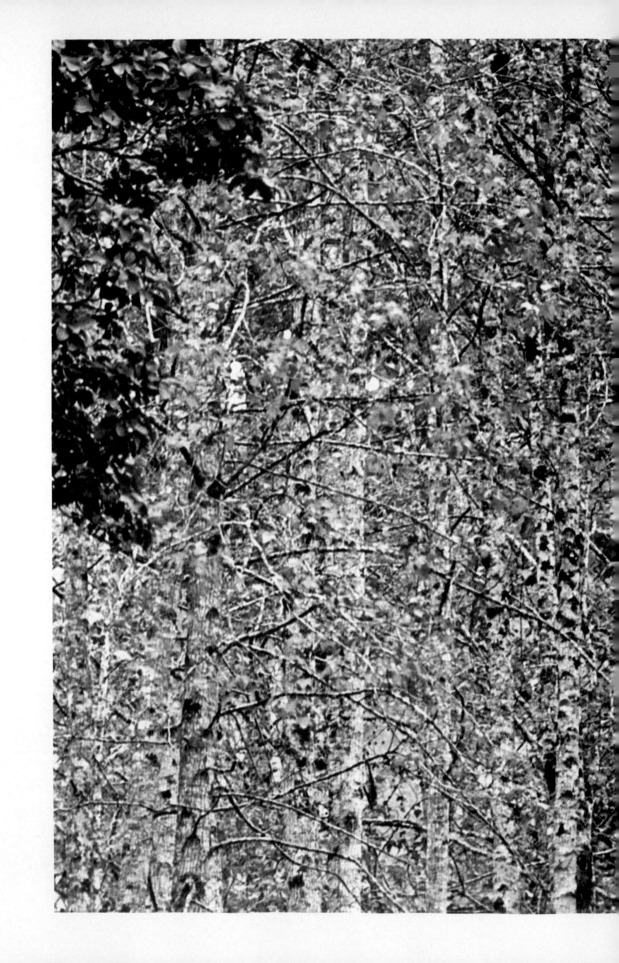

A STAND OF WHITE-BARKED SWEET GUM

FIG-TREE ROOTS CLUTCHING A LAVA BOULDER

NEEDLE CLUSTERS OF WHITE PINE

HAZE-SHROUDED RIDGES OF THE SIERRA DE LAS MINAS

Bibliography

Bates, Marston, *The Land and Wildlife of South America.* TIME-LIFE BOOKS, 1964.

Bustard, Robert, *Sea Turtles.* Taplinger Publishing Company, 1972.

Carr, Archie, *High Jungles and Low.* University of Florida Press, 1953.

Carr, Archie, *So Excellent a Fishe.* Natural History Press, 1967.

Carr, Archie, *The Windward Road.* Alfred A. Knopf, 1956.

Catalogue of the Active Volcanoes of the World, Part VI. The International Volcanological Association, 1958.

Ditmars, Raymond L., *Reptiles of the World.* Macmillan Company, 1933.

Dobson, Narda, *A History of Belize.* Longman Caribbean, 1973.

Hudson, William Henry, *Green Mansions.* Random House, 1944.

Lineaweaver, Thomas H., II, and Richard H. Backus, *The Natural History of Sharks.* J. B. Lippincott Company, 1970.

Mack, Gerstle, *The Land Divided.* Octagon, 1974.

Peterson, Roger Tory, and Edward L. Chalif, *A Field Guide to Mexican Birds.* Houghton Mifflin Company, 1973.

Richards, Paul W., *The Life of the Jungle.* McGraw-Hill Book Company, 1970.

Schneirla, T. C., *Army Ants.* W. H. Freeman and Company, 1971.

Skutch, Alexander F., *The Life of the Hummingbird.* Crown Publishers, 1973.

Slud, Paul, *The Birds of Costa Rica.* Vol. 128, Bulletin of The American Museum of Natural History, 1964.

Standley, Paul C., and Julian A. Steyermark, *Flora of Guatemala,* Vol. 24. Fieldiana: Botany, Chicago Natural History Museum, 1946.

Stephens, John L., *Incidents of Travel in Central America, Chiapas, & Yucatán,* 2 Vols. Rutgers University Press, 1949.

Thompson, J. Eric S., *The Rise and Fall of the Maya Civilization.* University of Oklahoma Press, 1977.

Walker, Ernest P., *Mammals of the World,* Vols. I and II. Johns Hopkins University Press, 1975.

Wauchope, Robert, gen. ed., *Handbook of Middle American Indians,* Vols. I, II and III. University of Texas Press, 1965.

Wilson, Edward O., *The Insect Societies.* Harvard University Press, 1971.

Periodicals and Papers

Britton, S. W., "Form and Function of the Sloth." *The Quarterly Review of Biology,* March 1941.

Brown, R. D., Jr., P. L. Ward and George Plafker, *Geologic and Seismological Aspects of the Managua, Nicaragua Earthquakes of December 23, 1972.* Geological Survey Professional Paper No. 838, U.S. Government Printing Office, 1973.

Carpenter, C. R., "A Field Study of the Behavior and Social Relations of Howling Monkeys." Unpublished paper.

Headley, J. T., "Darien Exploring Expedition." *Harper's New Monthly Magazine,* March 1855.

Krohn, Stewart, "Life in the Bush: Creepies and Crawlies, Long-leggedy Beasties and Cats That Roar in the Night," *Brukdown,* No. 6, 1978.

LaBastille, Anne, "Ecology and Management of the Atitlán Grebe, Lake Atitlán, Guatemala." *Wildlife Monographs* No. 37, August 1974.

Lundell, Cyrus Longworth, *The Vegetation of Peten.* No. 478, Carnegie Institution of Washington, 1937.

Marden, Luis, "A Land of Lakes and Volcanoes." *National Geographic,* August 1944.

Moynihan, M., *Some Behavior Patterns of Platyrrhine Monkeys.* Smithsonian Contributions of Zoology No. 28, Smithsonian Institution Press, April 1970.

Smith, Neal Griffith, "The Advantage of Being Parasitized." *Nature,* August 17, 1968.

Thorson, Thomas B., Donald E. Watson and C. Michael Cowan, "The Status of the Freshwater Shark of Lake Nicaragua." *Copeia,* September 7, 1966.

Willey, Gordon R., and Demitri B. Shimkin, "The Collapse of Classic Maya Civilization in the Southern Lowlands: A Symposium Summary Statement." *Southwestern Journal of Anthropology,* Spring 1971.

Acknowledgments

The author and editors of this book are particularly indebted to the following people: Archie Carr, Graduate Research Professor of Zoology, University of Florida, Gainesville; Daniel Janzen, Associate Professor of Zoology, University of Michigan, Ann Arbor; James Karr, Assistant Professor of Biology, Purdue University, Lafayette, Indiana; Thomas Thorson, Professor of Zoology, University of Nebraska, Lincoln; and Louis O. Williams, Curator Emeritus, Field Museum of Natural History, Chicago. They also wish to thank the following persons and institutions. In Belize: May Craig and Fred Keller, Belize City; Willie Faux, Placentia; Winston Miller and Iain Robertson, Fisheries Unit Laboratory, Belize City. In Costa Rica: Craig MacFarland, Centro Agronómico Tropical de Investigación y Enseñanza, Turrialba; In San José, Costa Rica: Mario Boza and Alvaro Ugalde, Ministry of Agriculture; Gary Hartshorn and David Janos, University of Costa Rica; Leslie Holdridge, George Powell and Joseph Tosi, The Tropical Science Center; The Organization for Tropical Studies, University of Costa Rica. In Guatemala: Edgar Bauer, Sololá; Pedro Castellano, Government Tourist Bureau, Flores. In Guatemala City: Roderico Anzueto, Robert Dorion and Luis de León, El Salto, S.A.; John Armstrong; Mario Dary, Universidad de San Carlos; Jorge Ibarra, Director, Museo Nacional de Historia Natural; Owen Smith. In Honduras: Antonio Molina, Escuela Agrícola Panamericana, Tegucigalpa. In Nicaragua: Antonio Flores, Juan Gazol and Jaime Incer, Managua; Kurt Koenig, Granada. In Panama: Stan Rand, Ira Rubinoff, Neal Smith and Nicholas Smythe, The Smithsonian Tropical Research Institution, Balboa. In Panama City: Carmen Arias and Audrey Kline, Instituto Panameño de Turismo; Pedro Galindo, Gorgas Memorial Laboratory; Robert Griffin. In New York: Anne LaBastille, Big Moose. In New York City: John Behler, Assistant Curator of Herpetology, and Donald F. Bruning, Associate Curator or Ornithology, New York Zoological Society; Sidney S. Horenstein, Department of Invertebrate Paleontology, The American Museum of Natural History; Larry G. Pardue, Plant Information Specialist, New York Botanical Garden. Also: Archie F. Carr III, University of Michigan, Ann Arbor; Howard Daughterty, Faculty of Environmental Studies, York University, Toronto, Canada; Curtis H. Freese and Paul Heltne, Johns Hopkins University, Baltimore, Maryland; Robert Holz, Department of Geography, University of Texas, Austin; Helen Kennedy, Department of Botany, National Museum of Natural History, Washington, D.C.; Ronald Liesner, Missouri Botanical Garden, St. Louis; Jeffrey McNeely, Commission on National Parks and Protected Areas, Gland, Switzerland; Kenton Miller, School of Natural Resources, University of Michigan, Ann Arbor; Luis Noriega, Guatemalan Embassy, Washington, D.C.; Fred and Jean Packard, Fairfax, Virginia; David Reynolds, International Affairs Branch, National Parks Service, Washington, D.C.; Donald Stone, Organization for Tropical Studies, Durham, North Carolina; James M. Stonehouse, Dartmouth College, Hanover, New Hampshire.

Picture Credits

Sources for the pictures in this book are shown below. Credits for pictures from left to right are separated by semicolons; from top to bottom by dashes.

The cover and all photographs are by Co Rentmeester except the following. End paper 4, page 1—Gibbs Milliken. 4, 5—David Hughes. 6, 7—Luis Villota. 8, 9 —Harvey Loomis. 10, 11—George Powell. 18, 19—Maps supplied by Hunting Surveys Limited. 22—David G. Allen. 26, 27—Don Moser. 32—Arthur A. Allen and David G. Allen. 49—Don Moser. 54, 55—George Holton. 56—Arthur A. Allen and David G. Allen. 61—Ricardo Mata. 62, 63—Jacques Jangoux. 66, 67 —Right Jacques Jangoux. 76—Ralph Holmes. 79—Daniel Janzen. 82, 83 —U. S. Army Engineers. 86—The New-York Historical Society. 91—John S. Dunning except top left and center The New York Zoological Society. 92—Carl Rettenmayer. 96—Ralph Holmes. 98—Nina Leen. 104, 105—N. Smythe from National Audubon Society—John D. Baldwin; N. Smythe. 106, 107—John Oppenheimer; Hladik from Jacana. 108, 109—John D. Baldwin; Hladik from Jacana. 112, 113—Bottom left David J. Chivers. 118 through 129 —Douglas Faulkner. 131—Don Moser. 144—Bottom Archie Carr. 146, 147 —Archie Carr except top right. 160 —N. Smythe.

Index

*Numerals in italics indicate a
photograph or drawing of the subject
mentioned.*